AF282633

Jan Fogfrost

Alcohol addiction on expert mode

Jan Fogfrost

Alcohol addiction on expert mode on expert mode

Copyright © 2023
by Books on Demand
Author: Jan Nebelfrost aka Jan Fogfrost

jannebelfrost@mailbox.org

Herstellung und Verlag: BoD – Books on Demand, Norderstedt

ISBN 9783757891640

Content

1. Introduction of the family

About myself: I liked to play with toy cars, had my own record player and also a cassette deck. I loved to listen to music. One day out father built a shelf in the children's room, to the left of the window. After a short time there was a personal computer on the shelf. First a Commodore VC-20, later a C-64. My father often hogged it for himself and typed pages of code from the magazine »64er«. So he typed code from the magazin for days, only to have a blue hot air balloon made of »sprites« fly back and forth on the monitor. The experience was very impressive for me. So i already saw at that time that you could do more with the »bread box« than just play games.

My brother, who is two years younger, never had any trouble in school, to my memory. It was not an issue for him. He had a rather normal stature. My stature, on the other hand, was more like Dad's. My brother Lothar quickly became interested in the sport of soccer. If you were looking for him, there weren't many options. You could either find him on the soccer field or on the soccer field near our neighborhood. I usally got along well with Lothar. We also often played together in the room with the toy cars or with play figures like »He-Man«. We often acted out scenes from the television series »Masters of the Universe«.

Mom was always hardworking and loving. Besides all the

household chores, she often had other work on the side. But she was also often away to earn money by cleaning. However, Mom always managed to keep the apartment clean. She was a real organizational talent. She used to learn the profession of soldering. Mom liked to knit or croche. And Mom liked to watch scary movies. One evening I secretly crept up to the entrance of the living room and lurked to the what Mom was watching on TV. And i saw on the TV how a man turned into a werewolf. As I learned years later, it was the movie »American Werewolf in London«. It was extremly scary for me and I quitly went back to bed. At night, I had a nasty nightmare. I woke up and cried. When mom came, I told her that I was lurking and she calmed me down.

Dad was tall and slim. He learned to be a car mechanic, but worked as a truck mechanic for a truck forwarding. He worked either early or late shifts. From time to time he was on call. As hobby he liked to tinker with model kits of the brand »Revell«. Beside aquaristics he was interested in electronics. Often he just soldered on small electronics parts for his models. His largest project and his pride and joy, was a landscape mounted on a wooden plate with of a model railroad. The panel was mounted behind the living room door and could simply be folded up or down. He often tried to get me interested in electronics. But electronics or electricity were never interesting to me.

Grandma and Grandpa from Dad's side were very, very

sweet and always obliging. Grandpa I had mostly sleeping on the couch in my memory. Grandma lovingly took care of Hansi the budgie. Grandpa and Grandma gave me a red BMX bike for my tenth birthday. They lived on the second floor directly on the street. There was a small garden with a cherry tree. Grandma often put grains in a small browl outside on the window sill for the birds. In colders seasons she hung titmouse dumplings in the garden. In general, she always had something for the birds. When visitors came at the weekend, there was a shot of brandy for the adults. I always found the smell interesting. Often, as a little boy, I tried to drink the leftovers. Sometimes the adults couldn't stop me because I did it surprisingly fast. So there was a little gag made of it. In the walk-in attic, I and my cousin Tatjana played very often.

Grandma and Grandpa from Mom's side were also always very, very sweet. They lived on a farm, but also moved to another farm once. In the past grandma and grandpa had cows, pigs, wolfdogs, chickens, geese, ponies and german shepard dogs. Since my mom had a total of twelve siblings, there was always quite a lot going on at the farm. On weekends, other relatives or acquaintances came to visit. And then grandpa would say to one of his older children »Come on, get the carriage ready, we're going for a ride or two«. So then the carriage was brought out and grandpa then drove us kids through the peasantry. That was really great. I was the oldest grandson and so grandpa would always show me jokes, like how he'd tease others in a nasty way.

Grandpa was a heavy chain smoker and usally smoked four packs a day. Once he was sitting in the big living room and I was sitting next to him – we were watching TV. He lit a cigarette and waited until his daugther Hilde came. Hilde often walked back and forth and was an extremly restless person. When she came, he suddenly ashes on the carpet and shouted »Come on, Hilde! Get the vacuum cleaner! Someone has ash here!« Grandma and Hilde always cooked together for everyone and were a well-rehearsed team.

Once, when I was about eight or nine, Grandpa took me out back to the meadow by the ponies. He called a pony over and said »Go on, sit on it. You can go for a ride.« I didn't suspect and swung myself onto the pony. Then Grandpa just said »Hold on to the mane!« and as soon as I grabbed it, he gave the pony a big slap on the butt. The pony galloped with me through the meadow and I was fully scared to fly down. The pony calmed down relativly quickly and stopped after half a round across the meadow. Crazy.

2. Introduction of relatives

My cousin Tatjana, that is, the daughter of Dad's sister, was my best friend. She was a little older than me and always played with me when we were at Grandma's house. She liked to play with Barbie dolls and listen to music, just like me. We would swing each other in a hammock. We picked cherries together in Grandma's garden and drew roads on the concrete floor with chalk. We listened to the songs of the new German wave together. Tatjana was one of the most important people of my childhood – without her knowing it. It was a very familiar bond. I always got along well with her younger brothers. I also played with them when they visited Grandma. But not as much as with my cousin.

I could only play with the children of my mother's siblings when we went to the farm. But we were there less often than at my grandma's in the city. But here it was also fun, because the toys were completly different. Of course, there was also much more space. Outside we could drive around with small toy tractors and »play« farm. Of course, it was also cute to look at all the animals. Also the whole nature around was very inviting to discover. So we found species of insects that we could would encounter in an apartment on the second floor rather rarely to not at all.

We stayed there on weekends in a seperate room for guests. In the winter months it was often so very cold that they put a radiator in our room. To go to sleep, we received a hot water bottle to take to bed with them so that we could fall asleep better and not catch a cold. We were often so many children that we had to eat at several tables. There was often grandma's perfect barley soup. The taste of this good barley soup immortalized itself in my brain.

3. Kindergarden time

I felt like a normalboy at first. Only in tall with long, thin legs. My long, skinny stature looked funny. And because I was so tall, the other kids thought it was an unfair advantage. Some gt jealous and started teasing me. How could being teased be an advantage? In kindergarden, I learned how to feel afterwards. So there were ncie moments in kindergarden. But the biggest memories were rather sad. Because of my long, thin stature, I was called a beanpole. That hurt a lot and made me suspicious. Once at carnival I was dressed up as a woman. It was no problem, so I wanted to be a part of the group. And be happy, not sad all the time. I often wished my size had been an advantage. It was just the opposite. I was the tallest, but was »punished« with almost daily teasing. Once when we were sitting in a circle, everyone was supposed to divide their first name into syllables with a bell. When it was my turn, I sang »Ja – han.« That was wrong, of course, the correct name would have been Jan. I was ashamed that I couldn't manage this task.

The teasing often came secretly and unpredictably. From the second year on, a great fear developed. Fear of teasing that I mighted have to endure again in kindergarden. I did not know if and when it would happen again. But I lived through the deep-seated fear every day. I developed the strategy for myself to be as much as possible for myself. In no case to be in the focus and to stand out. This was difficult to keep up as a big kid in kindergarden. It was exactly this task that got me down inside. So I showed as little emotion as possible. I wanted to show that I didn't mind. I didn't want to show that it hurt me. And if it did happen, it hit me hard. But still I pretended that I didn't care. I carried the sad moments in my head and heart home with me and pushed them aside very, very often, with very, very much music. Music helped me the best.

4. Memories from childhood

We lived in a relativly small high-rise building. For a town like Brokolt, this high-rise building with its three or four floors was not particulary striking. We lived in the second floor. Each floor had three apartments, We lived in the middle. Down in the front of the door, the street made the next left turn after about 25 meters. Exactly in the middle of the bend there was a path to the soccer field. On the way to the soccer field there were also small apartments on the right. In one of the apartments lived at that time also one of two friends with whom I rode BMX.

Therefore I called the two friends my BMX friends. One of the two showed me on our street how to ride on the back tire. Or how to jump down a slope at the soccer field. After that came gravel and only a few meters further lawn. One day when I was practicing jumping down, the front wheel slid to the side when I touched down and before I flew down, one of the hand grips hit me in the stomach. This was not good at all. Staggering slightly, I pushed myself and my bike home.

With our BMX bikes, we very often boarded through the forest. There was a good path to ride through with the BMX. I also dared to go into industrial area alone after a few times. At the weekend there was an opportunity to drive really fast on the wide streets without being disturbed. One curve had done it to me. I thought that I knew this one curve so well that I could drive through it and look behind. No sooner said than done. I took a good-run-up and then simply looked behind me before the bend. I was much too fast, briefly noticed the elevationof the parking lot and »BAM«. I flew against the drawbar of a trailer. The BMX flew under the drawbar through and I a bit of a stomachache.

 When I was at Grandma's in townm I always had a red folding bike there to ride. I liked to ride my bike. And so I used to ride the bikde diligently around the block. Later, I exlored the neighborhood a little more. I also liked to watch television. I loved to watch »A Colt for All Seasons«, »Master of the Universe« or »Knight Rider«. The car was so modern, with all these futuristic buttons. I drew the buttons on the cardboard and then glued them to the steering wheel of the BMX bike. There I was in my role. I was cool. I even dreamed once that »K.I.T.T.« would come and pick me up. Completly crazy. With my brother I often played »He-Man« and »Skeletor«. The were toy figures from the brand »Mattel«. We had a few figures of them ans the two castles. One for »He-Man« and one for »Skeletor«. Of course, I always wanted to be the blond, strong He-Man.

 We shared the room. I was mighty proud of my music system. Only the music was often the same. So i was really infatuated with »Modern Talking« or »Falco«. Later music of »Michael Jackson« followed. Very often I listened to the records of »Otto Waalkes« (a german comedy star and actor) or of »Mike Krüger« (german actor and musician). The songs to a perfomance of »Otto Waalkes« could later be bought on record. the neighbor boy from upstairs sometimes showed me newer music, so that I at least halfway knew what was trendy.

I also remembered very strongly a vacation trip with the family to Oberhausen. I had a relative there, but I had only seen her once before. At the time I was still listening to »Modern Talking«, because I really liked the music. When we were there, she showed me her music collection. And it came as it had to come. She showed me records of »Die Toten Hosen« (german punk rock band« and »Die Ärzte« (called »the doctors«, also a german punk rock band). I was shocked at my backlog in music and woke up. From then on, I thought to myself »I'm always looking at new music instead of focusing on a specific style of music.« I adopted this way of thinking later in life for the other senses as well.

5. Criminal energy in the kiosk

In the kiosk, which I always visited, I soon discovered a peculiarity. There were three indentations in the store on the left side in the back. In the last one were boxes of candy. One took out what one wanted to buy. At that time there were no mirrors or cameras there either. If you stood in the last bay, you were not seen from the front. So I took a few pennies with me a few times and went into the kiosk. Pennies were in the old currency, like cents today. There I went to the candy shelf in the back and pretend to be indecisive. But in reality, I used the time to put some candy in my pocket.

But only so many that it wasn't noticeable. The I took the ones I really wanted to buy and went to the checkout with them. At first, there were only a few. After a few test purchases, I used as many pockets of my clothes as possible. later, the thrill grew. The more I took out, the biggest the thrill became. When I couldn't get my opckets full enough, I asked my brother Lothar to come along. On the way to the kiosk, I explained my tactics to him. We entered the kiosk and went to the back. Everyone pocketed various things. Among other things, »surprise eggs« (german chocolate eggs with a toy).

I took some more candy to the front for the cash register and paid. Back outside, we walked a few meters and sat down on a wall by the road. Excitedly, we unpacked our common booty. All of sudden, there were lots and lots of sweets. It happened at that very moment. For me it happend in slow motion. Mom approached from the left with the car. I froze in shock. There was also no time left to hide loot or part sof it. Lothar looked at me questioningly, but we were sitting there like birds on a perch. Between the two of us lay all the stuff. As we passed, she first looked at the candy. Then her scutinizing gaze turned to my eyes. I will never forget that look. What a bummer, I thought. What a akward moment.

If only I had chosen a smarter place. Arrived at home, I quickly went to my room and suspected nothing good. Lothar stayed in front. He couldn't help it, I had put him up to it. My mom was furious and scolded loudly. »Wait until Dad comes home!«. And he did come home. I first heard Mama tell him what happened. Then I heard his heavy, pounding footsteps getting louder and louder. Like an earthquake toward the nursery. The door flew open, he looked at me for a moment and slapped me hard. »Grounded for a month! No musc and no computer!« He left and pulled the door shut. Later, Mom came back to me and asked why I was doing this. We would get pocket money, after all. But what should I say? At the time, I didn't really know why I loved stealing so much. So I remained silent. After all, I had already caused enough worry with my bad grades. At that age, I could not yet know that the thrill could also become an addiction. So I distracted myself for the month with various toys like the toy cars. But during that time, I also rethought m tactics. From now on, it always had to be done in such a way that the prey could not be seen in any case.

6. Playing with fire

There was a day when I was looking for some excitement. Mom and Dad sat clueless in the living room. I wanted to try an experiment. All the stuffed animals were made of different materials. So I asked myself »Which material would burn the fastest?« A really crazy question. But such things used to go through my mind. So I went into the living room under false pretext and secretly stole a lighter. Back in the children's room, I pulled the door shut. When we played in the room, the door was actually always closed. For our parents, this was an absoloutly harmonious state of affairs. I took advantage of that this time and let Lothar in on it. He asked me extra »Isn't that dangerous?« I suggested the following »You hold the stuffed animal. I light it briefly and then blow it out again immediately.« With that, I was able to calm him down and he agreed.

We put all the stuffed animals on our brown toy cabinet. Before we begin, I open the window so the smoke could flow straight out. Now Lothar always took a stuffed animal and held it out to me. I always lit it in a rather inconspicuous place, observed briefly whether and how quickly the flame spread. Then I blew it out again. Soon we were done. After that, all the stuffed animals had a round spot where something was missing. Fortunately, our parents did not notice. Since it was the weekend, they took me to Grandma's in the city in the afternoon. Where I was allowed to sleep again. The next morning, Grandma's ohone rang. It was Dad's turn and excitedly told Grandma that there had been a fire at home. Dad was coming to pick me up right away.

I put on my cap (like Colt Seavas in »A Colt for all seasons«) and found myself in the role of a stuntman. I thought, now I would get the chance to save my own brother from the flames. What crazy thoughts. My dad picked me up and we drove home. On the drive, Dad told me that Lothar must have been playing with fire. Lothar lit something and was startled to see that the flames spread very quickly. So he ran out, closed the door and hid under our parents' bed. Dad woke up to the sound of brunfing things collapsing. He also noticed the smell of smoke. Instinctively, but of course in panic, he jumped up and opened the door of the room, where flames were already flying towards him. Fortunately, we had a water connection in the hallway on the second floor and a garden hose.

Dad put out the fire all by himself. He told me on the way to the apartment, »No matter what the questions, you have nothing to do with it. You know nothing.« When we arrived, the fire brigade was already there, checking what had happened. There were still hot spots that could have reignited the fire. Then I saw Lothar and his empty look. The look that said something like »How can I ever trust you again?« I saw our room, or rather what was left of it. Everything was black and charred. Everything was sooty and no longer usable. Even my keyboard was lying there. Charred and completly bent. Then I understood that it is not good to show younger children how to play with fire.

7. Judo club

When I first started thinking up exciting experiments on my own, I still thought that was fine. But the more I realized they were backfiring, thoughts circulated about my own actions. Why did I often seek out risk? Why did I think stealing was good? What was I thinking, inciting my brother Lothar to steal or set things on fire? Since I was lousy at school, I needed something to compensate. Which acted on me like a reward. A feeling where I could feel joy. And I got that feeling when I stole for myself and didn't get caught. By taking my brother to steal, I wanted to reinforce that feeling. Now it backfired here. And even after playing with fire, I wondered very often if I wasn't just a bad person. I was bad at school. Bad to my brother. Bad to my parents. Bad for others, too, apparently especially for those who teased me at school almost every day.

 Our mom realized that it would be good if we know how to fight back. So she enrooled us in the judo club. And we were training there for a few weeks. The daughter of the judo coach appealed to me visually. But I was emotionally broken at the time, my psyche was completely off track. Sometimes happy, sometimes sad. When I was once again waylaid by a classmate after school, i fought back for the first time in my life. After he said something nonsensical and tried to attack me, I kicked him in the stomach and ran home. With the judo club we even went to an event in

24

Oberhausen once. This was a nice time in itself. Until I went crazy again. There is no other way to describe it. On the weekend I and my cousin Tatjana were again with our grandma in the city. Grandma went shopping. And we fooled around. I told Tatjana about the judo teacher's daughter. Somehow we got the idea to call her. And I was a daring idiot, yakking really obscenes things on the tape. Simply shameful. Allusions that a father certainly wouldn't want to hear on the answering machine.

No sooner had I hung up the phone than I had an inkling of what was to come. Monday. A call at our house from the judo club. Mom and I were to come over immediately. I was scared and knew what was coming. Mom had no idea. So we went in and I was still somehow falsely hoping for the trainer's indulgence. But it wasn't. He said to my mom »Here listen!« Then he promptly ignited the bomb and pressed the play button of the answering maschine. I heard myself and the things I said. I felt ashamed and just looked for the hole to jumped in. I couldn't look the coach in the eye anymore. Then he said »I do not condone such misconduct. And that's why I can't train you anymore. Please leave.« My mom looked at me again so dissappointed and we walked out. Must this have been a nasty moment for my mom. We drove home. Mama expected a lot but it was a real shame. At home there were some conversations about this again. Questions like »Why did you do that?«, »Do you want people to think badly of us?«, »Aren't you ashamed of yourself?« I didn't know that myself. I've often done things without thinking much about the consequences.

Through these actions I compensated for negative states. This also became an addiction, only I did not yet know what addiction meant. I created a good feeling for myself for a moment. No matter what came. In retrospect, forbidden actions and the thrill were a kind of comfort. I saw no other options for myself. So I already had a bad image additionally about all the teasing I had been going through for some time. A downward spiral: the bad grades, all the lousy actions. That's how a learning block came about. So for far too long I kept quiet about tha fact that I was sad because of the recurring hidden teasing. This created a daily fear of going to school. Because of this reason, I couldn't concentrate in class. Because I was way too busy watching to see if anyone was teasing about me. I was very often in a bad mood about the lousy grades in school. With this sadness, I spent a lot of time with listen music in our room. On a top of that, the fear of coming around the corner to my parents with even more baggage. Trying to learn was a race against time for me. And so I often asked myself »What am I and all this good for?«

8. Childhood accidents

One day, Mom had to send a package urgently. She drove to the post office with me and Lothar. I was about eight years old and my brother was six. The environment in the post office was boring for us, so we played tag. We ran through the post office and Lothar chased me. There I slipped and banged my head very hard against a ribbed radiator. I howled and had a laceration on my head. None of the people present helped Mom or me. Mom then had to drive very quickly to the hospital with me and Lothar so that my wound could be treated. Fortunately, it looked worse than it actually was. The wound healed without complications.

A break in the elementary school. I went to a step pyramid, build of round wooden beams and climbed up. Almost at the top, I hit one of the wooden beams hard with my right knee. It didn't hurt and I was wondering. Then, without any sign, I felt sick and then blacked out. I woke up was suddenly lying on a stretcher in the first aid room of the school. A teacher told me I had fainted and asked me how I was doing. Before I could answer properly, I blacked out again. When I woke up this time, I was sitting next to Mom on the car. Probably direction family doctor or hospital. I fainted again. When I woke up fo this time, I was lying in bed at home. At school, I fell down from the scaffolding in a faint. Like a wet sack. When I fell down, I hit my head again.

We drove to grandma's in the city. On the way there, I got serve stomach ache. When we got there, Dad parked the car on the right side on the road. There were many trees there. I was so preoccupied with my stomach ache that I wasn't paying attention when I got out of the car and ran straight into a tree. With stomach pain and scratched face I lay later with grandma on the couch. A few visits to the toilet relieved me. The stomach pain slowly went away. One day I overslept and rushed to the school. I was really late. When I arrived at the school, I took the shortcut across the square where the bicycles were parked. So I meandered through there and just had to hop over an iron chain. The iron chain was connected to posts on the left and right and seperated this square from the schoolyard.

I ran up and jumped. Unfortunately, because of the weight of the satchel, I couldn't jump high as I thought I could. So the weight of the satchel increased my body weight at the wrong moment. I caught one foot in the chain and hit the hard ground headfirst. After I picked myself up, I ran into the school in a panic. I opened the door to the class and screamed out the pain. Everyone flinched. The teacher quickly took me to the first aid room. A walnut-sized bruise was forming on the right side of my forehead and was about to burst. It was extremly painful and I was crying. My mother picked me up from school again at this extraordinary time and drove me to the hospital. There they cooled the wound and I was glad that it did nut burst. Since then I never jumped over such a chain again.

Winter: I and some other kids went into the forest and wanted to go sledding. At the top of a mountain, one of the fellows came up with the idea of connecting five sleds together. We connected the five sledges and drove down the mountain The ride began. I was the last tethered candidate. It was going downhill quite steeply and good speed was developing. Then my sled drifted off the right with me – towards a tree. However, since I was tied to the sled of the candidate in front and thus to all the others, I could not brake. I slammed with the sled full against the tree, my face banged on the bark. My face was covered in blood. One of the colleagues brought me and the sled home.

9. Learning to swim

In Brokolt, where we grew up, there was a large lake and a beach where people met in the summer. To doze, to sunbathe or even to learn how to swim. At that lake we used to meet with grandma and grandpa and feel like we were on vacation. I also learned to siwm there. Once my brother climbed onto an air mattress near the beach and started paddling in the water. It didn't take long, however, before he came to an area where the water was far too deep for him. My brother Lothar couldn't swim back then, so the situation was very tricky.

Fortunately, Dad noticed it in time and jumped into the water like a lifeguard to bring him back. We have been to the lake many times. For us this was a wonderful place where we could play well. Later, at school, I could already swim. I couldn't swim very well, but it was easily enough for the Seahorse. In general, sports were never my thing. That's why I had to got to gymnastics tutoring every Thursday in elementary school in the 3rd or 4th grade. And that was very uncomfortable and humiliating for me as the only boy.

10. Divorce of parents

Mom was shopping and only Dad and I were at home. I was doing math homework. At that time, one of my parents always checked my homework. Since only Dad was there, I could only show it to him. So I went to the front part of the apartment, to the living room to Dad and showed him my (apparently) solved homework. He just said »Not right« and I didn't know what he meant. I went back to the nursery and looked over it again. To me, I didn't see a mistake. I just didn't see one. So I went back to the front and again he just said »That's not true. Check again.« I went back into the room again and checked for me the assinment with the personal ccomputer. And also there I got out what I already had as a solution. Of course I coud have made a mistake. But why didn't my own father explain it to me?

I was dissapointed and sad at the same time. I had no chance. Since I saw no mistake and also got no help, I felt even more left alone in my small world. Maybe my dad would finally show me what was wrong in the third attempt? I had great doubts, but also no other possibilities to find out. Now I gathered all my courage, my great fear and went to Him for the third time. My daad looked things again and unfortunately said again »That's not so.« Again without giving me even slightest bit of help. There was nothing. Nothing at all. The moment he said it again, I just felt empty in my mind and body.

I walked slowly back to the nursery in a daze. My head felt like someone was smothering me with a pillow. I felt unloved und unwanted. Like a mistake. As if he doesn't want me and shows me that by sending me away again and again. Like at school, where I was teased over and over again.And felt not wanted. How could I stand by myself when even my own dad kept sending me away? Inside me I felt so unwanted and useless that I just didn't want to bear it any longer. At the time, the skyscrapper was being renovated from the outside and there was scaffolding on the wall. So I opened the window and climbed onto the window sill on the second floor. I was about to climb onto the scaffolding when the door of the children's room opened. Mom saw me and startled. Then she came up to me, pulled me down and closed the window. I stayed in the room and she angrily went to the front and they both argued very, very violently. Again I was afraid and had the feeling that I was only bringing bad things. My father probably saw it rather calmly. At least that's how it seemed to me.

That day we didn't talk much anymore with each other. For me, it was as if I were the guilt in person. Once again, I was the one who brought in this unrest. The next day, as I was walking up the stairs after school, a neighbor's daughter suddenly looked down and shouted, »Your mommy has fallen in love with our daddy!« The neighbor was a single father with two daughters. There I already thought that today something will change significantly. Mom then guided me upstairs directly to the neighbor and explained the situation. He helped Mom to get a place in the mother-child home. So we would move out for good. I asked Mama if she had thought of my keyboard (Yamaha). So there was no relationship or anything. The daughter just couldn't describe it any other way. She probably understood it that way because our mom confided in him. Mom explained to us that we – that is, Mom, my brother and I would seperate from Dad. And this mother-child home was a protected place where we would not have to be afraid.

One of mom's sisters picked us up and drove us to the mother-child home. And the whole thing before Dad had finished work. Of course, I also took my BMX bike with me. In the late afternoon, they both went to the parking lot and dad started talking to mom. Both went to the parking lot and Dad began to talk to Mom. I rode the BMX bike around the two of them. Mom was silent all the time. She simply remained silent and crossed both arms instead of saying out loud what she was thinking. Probably it would now have been good to address these issues aloud. At some point I said, »Come on, Mom, now say something!« But Mom remained silent. Dad left after about 20 minutes. Mom was visibly relieved and we went to the mother-child home. Our family no longer existed. We no longer lived together or went anywhere together. I never forgot that day. I changed elementary schools. Maybe it made it easier for me to deal with the school because the children there didn't know me. But I couldn't just turn off my fear of being teased. In the mother-child home I began to build up my rebellious phase.

After a few days, I wondered how Dad was doing and just wanted to visit him. I knew he was at Grandma's most of the time, so one afternoon I just walked there. I have not discussed this trip around the city with anyone before. And so there was a lot of worry when I arrived. As soon as Grandma let me in, Dad said »Boy, it's great that your're here, but you can't be here! You have to go back, because otherwise they'll think I think I just took you with me.« I hadn't thought of that. And again, I was semmeingly unwanted. At least that's how I felt. To that time, there was still no regulation on the subject of visitation ritghs. So they brought me back to the mother-child home. A few days later I took 20 German marks from my pocket money and my Walkman with the music of Michael Jackson. And just walked into the city. The big bus station attracted me magically.

Apparently there were like-minded people there. People met here who were apparently unwanted elsewhere. I bought beer from punks and I got cigarettes too. Here I began to drink and smoke. I immediately felt understood. Apparently, each of these people had similar problems to mine. So I drank and smoked until I was completely inebriated when I was taken back to the mother and child home by a man in a car later that day. So I sat drunk in the smoking room in the late afternoon. And I deliberately lit a cigarette in front of my mother. For her it was my first cigarette. Not for me.

11. From farm to ghetto

After a few month in the mother-child home, we were able to move in with grandma and grandpa on the farm. Here, too, I changed schools again. The school material was again foreign to me. Attending school was simply a compulsory event for me. Without any claim to a good grade. This was only an emergency solution, since it was not yet clear where we could move. On the farm uncle Thobass showed me what real rock music is. He played me all kinds of different genres and showes me how to build an amplifier out of and old record player. On the farm there was just quite a mess, because there the heating system was completly renovated. Accordingly, many realtives helped here. Among them was a man who seemed to like Mama. It only took a few days for the two of them to get together. Mom asked us if we would agree if he would be our new dad. We didn't have much other choice and he was quite nice and funny. He was a skilled head butcher and could help out anywhere.

We had a lot of fun together during the time on the farm, there were always so many people and it was often very busy. Many acquaintances and relatives came and no sooner had one visitor left than the next one came in. A few weeks later we moved – so mom, our new stepfather, my brother and to the small sommunity of Schöningen. Schöningen is located in the western part of Germany. Unfortunately, we lived in a socially deprived area. Here lived those who earned only little, mediocre or nothing at all. Further up the hill – at least that's what those from the socially deprived area thought – lived the better earners, the rich. The new stepfather could no longer accept a normal job because of his back pain and quite soon applied for early retirement. Financially, we were soon dependent on the social welfare office. Again there was a change of school. Here I started in the fifth grade of the secondary schools. And as it looked, this would probably work a little longer.

So I began, despite my fears of taunts, to just pull myself together and get through it. Through the court, the divorce process between mom and dad was underway. Dad got visitation rights, which meant that Dad was allowed to pick us up in the morning one day and had to bring us home again in the evening. Dad brought me the personal computer and picked me and my brother Lothar up more often on Saturday or Sunday. Slowly I got to know the people in the neighborhood. There was no internet yet, so it was common to just walk out the front door or walk around the neighborhood to look around.

I first got to know Rainer through the school. He was a class above me and lived next door. Rainer liked to play with game consoles and even had several of them. He also often played with his father. His father was an extreme chain smoker of filterless cigarettes of the brand called »Overstolz« (of course without filter). A very strong variety.

So sometimes you would stand downstairs between the houses and hear someone upstairs lose »Such a fucking shit here!!!« followed by the sound of one of the many joysticks flying into a wall and splitting. We often stood down between the houses and then had to laugh, because that happened really often. So I was more often just after school at Rainer´s and played with him. After a few days I also met Keith in front of the door. The street that seperated the houses was only so wide that at most one car could drive here.

Sooner or later you inevitably met and got to know each other. Keith was two years older than me and had a visual impairment. Because of the handicap, his line of sight always wandered slowly from one side to the other. Which is why he was often teased as »K.I.T.T.« or »Knight Rider«. It referred to the scanner light on the car. I was never bothered by his disability. We exchanged ideas about computers, consoles and hobbies. We hit it off right away and he invited me to his house. Keith had two younger brothers, one of whoom he shared a room with. He showed me what he listened to for music and watched for movies. Like me, Keith was a fan of horror movies. So he showed me among other things VHS film cassettes of »A Nightmare on Elm Street«. Keith grew up in Munster, more precisely in the Munster »Kinderhaus« neighborhood, and like me he did not have a good childhood. As I later learned from Keith, his childhood was not free from violence. His father was also a severe alcoholic. With his mother and brothers, he lived with a woman who gave the family the opportunity to live there as well. I got along with Keith right away and we became friends. Keith already knew Rainer.

Keith also knew deaf language because he attended the Westphalian School for the Visually Impaired and Blind. I only knew something like that from TV. Keith always met me at eye level. And he was good at putting himself in other´s people shoe´s. Word of my interest in computers spread quickly. At school, I sold printed banners on continuous paper. For example, with lettering like »Helloween« between two pumpkin heads. The computer hobby was very high on my list. Rainer also got a personal computer later. I was ver happy when I got a new keyboard for one of my birthdays. It was a Yamaha model PSS-480, a keyboard with a built-in digital FM synthesizer. That was something. For me a very futuristic part. One of the schoolmates, who lived at the beginning of the street, thaught me three songs. His father was a solo entertainer, so his son, my schoolmate, could play the keyboard. As soon as we had visitors, I always had to play these three songs. How terrible. It wasn't long before there was techno and hip-hop too.

I soon got to know Oskar through Rainer. He lived high up on the mountain with his parents. I also became friends with him. But he was already a bit older. He showed me how to copy computer games very quickly. Or how to install a microphone connection to the cassette part of the C64. Also later schoolmate showed me how to use special fonts in the C64 for demos. But how exactly that worked, I didn't understand yet. I didn't have anything like a permanent teacher. Instead, I limited myself to a manageable amount of copied games. For me, the intros to the games were usually more interesting than the games as such. I also liked to just look at demos and enjoy the music. The demoscene got interesting for me. Up to this point, a lot of things went well for me. Except for the disastrous school performance. I began to drink beer secretly often after school. Also during the week. Also alone. I've tried over and over again to wash away all the past. The periods when I drank became more frequent. After school or on weekends, too.

With fifteen I then obtained my driving license for a moped and my real dad then even gave me a used moped. He brought the blue Vespa Ciao on a trailer over. He downloaded the moped and I immediately went for a test drive. Once up and down the street. Since the mood between the stepfather and my real dad was not particularly good, my dad then drove again quite quickly. Now I even had a moped! When we lived about 6 month in the village, When we lived in the village for about 6 months, Mamma got a bit fat and I just asked if she was pregnant. Mom couldn´t deny it and said »Now it´s come out!«. I couldn´t yet imagine what it would be like with a baby brother, so I just let it come to us. Shortly before the baby brother was born, named Elias, I had to clear out my room upstairs. In the last room in the basement on the right, the stepfather covered the walls with wood paneling. And a rug came in. There was no heating there. But it wasn´t particularly cold either. In my basement room I had a bed, a computer table and a couch. So I could play on my computer or make music with the keyboard in peace.

I once played the computer game Elite with Keith all night in my basement. A space game. One of the first games with real three-dimensional graphics. It was only black and white, but it was really fun. Together with bags of chips and Coke, we were able to get through the night just fine. Keith became a really goof friend for me, whom I could confide in.

It was summer and I was behind the house when a local girl approached me. She wanted to go camping with me. I said of course not no. The tent was set up very quickly. Later wa lay in the tent and a light thunderstorm came up. She said she was afraid of a thunderstorm and asked if we could go to my room in the basement. The next morning I went upstairs to get something for breakfast. When I came downstairs, she was just gone. How mean! But well. It was just the way it was. Dissapointed, I ate breakfast alone. Diagonally apposite also lived two girls. I liked one of them very much and wanted to »go together« with her. It took a

41

few days and then I almost got together with her. But we didn't make out yet. Keith, on the other hand, had in the meantime moved from Bonnerstreet a few streets away to the old farmhouse behind the soccer club.

Across the street there was also a shelter for refugees and people who needed support. But he was always a little different, like the others in a sarcastic sense. Purely as a precautionary measure, he bought a »slightly« oversized blanking pistol. The gun was beautiful silver color. He occasionally fired a few shots in the dark in the middle of the ghetto at a late hour for fun. To make the neighbors cringe. We just liked it. We wanted that American feel. Then came New Year´s Eve and I was with Bob, another colleague from the ghetto in the basement and we were listening to music by »Iron Maiden«. Then Berti (another colleague) came to visit and said that Keith had taken my pearl (girlfriend). There I became furious. I went out with Berti as a backup and went with him out of the ghetto to Keith. His door was open a crack, so I opened the door and started screaming. Berti calmed me down. I just wanted to show that I'm not going to let this get away with me. Keith was lying in bed in his own vomit at first, but then he woke up. That´s when he took the magazine from the pistol, but failed miserably trying to fill it. The comedy of the situation almost made a hit. But we were also drunk. Here I was very disappointed in him. After I loudly defended my point of view, we left again. Berti went his way and I cried at Rainer´s basement party. That´s just the way it was.

Legendary memory of a video evening to which my aunt (sister of mom) and uncle, me together with another uncle, had invited. There was a really good selection of alcoholic drinks, but also cola and lemonade. I want my glass of probably five different alcoholic beverages with false pride. We toasted and I drank about half of the glass. After about half an hour, I became very, very warm. I drank some more and actually the preview was still playing. But for me, the movie was already on. I no longer really knew what I had done. Only that I slowly became funny and asked if that was already the film with the »Chainsaw Massacre« would be. I didn´t get anything more from the film, but somehow sank down inside me. Then I blacked out.

When I woke up, I was suddenly lying on a sleeping mat, covered with a sleeping bag. I felt really, really felt like shit. I was so sick that I couldn´t move at first. My head was so full, as if there was a very thick block in it and the skull was about to burst. And it was already almost noon. Then I heard my uncles yell »Come on, Jan! Breakfast's ready!« Then I got up with a lot of effort and dragged myself to the table. I was told that they almost wanted to drive me to the hospital because I had stopped responding. Even a cold shower would not have helped. So they undressed me – while I had my blackout – and »packed« me under the shower. That helped a little and they put my dressed on the slepping mat and covered me up. I should try to eat something. I was still so nauseous. It felt as if my brain was going to spin all the time and it idn´t stop. I tried to get back on the corner seat. »No Jan, come on stay seated!« – I heard. After another hour or so, the dizziness subsided somehat, but was still not gone. The uncle drove me home, where the stepfather was already waiting for me. »Oh look! The prodigal son is back again. You can come right in and flush!« The uncle wished me good luck and drove away.

Then I was allowed to wash dishes directly, because we didn´t have a dishwasher. I staggered back and forth a few times. That must have looked funny to my parents. But a few minutes later I had made it. I thought I could finally rest downstairs in the room, but I didn´t count in my stepfather »You can also tidy up and ventilate downstairs!« So I went downstairs, grabbed the street broom and basically swept my carpet. That was the quickest and most effective way to keep things tidy around here. Since I wanted to finish quickly, I hurried. I was starting to feel dizzy again and yanked a leg off the bed with the broom. »Crack!« The bed banged on the floor because the one wooden leg was now missing. I had to temporarily craft a stone underneath. By the time I finally got the room cleand up, it was late afternoon. I was just glad that the dizziness was subsiding. On my nightstand, I always had little tea lights like this as a light. In the evening I just wanted to sleep and a tea light burned for an unusually long time.

That's enough, I thought to myself, and simply spat on the tea light from above. Suddenly, lots of burning dots flew around me. And I didn't know why. I was scared of death. Fortunately, I didn't burn myself. But there were little wax dots all over the place.

When the first brother Elias came into the world, the chaos started. Since I consider Elias like a real brother, I helped to take care of him. And to do the chores that come with it, like changing diapers. I was not always happy with the situation, but still had to get through it. The stepfather was still quite funny at the time, but could also get really serious. At the time I just wanted to go out and play. Do what I wanted to do. Uncle Thobass slept here with us for a few days, because he had no other place to stay at the time. He showed me what the disc or a pinion on a moped could be important for. To make the moped faster, of course! Thobass smoked, too. From time to time I puffed a cigarette from him or could roll one. The girl who stayed with me knew – no wonder – other boys from the village and introduced me to them. I asked her because I heard the topic of marihuana was making the rounds. In the truest sense of the word.

But I had no idea about marihuana or how to roll a joint. She invited me to smoke a pseudo joint with tea. At the end of the road there were three forests: the first was right at the beginning, then there was a field, then came the second forest. And then another field and then the third forest. We went to the second forest. There she built a real improvised dowel with tobacco and tea inside. And we smoked that thing. She said to me that this tasters about the same as real smoking. Yes well, there I became again a little dizzy. But I had to admit to myself: It attracted me magically already very, very.

12. It became wild

I no longer knew exactly how the next, described meeting in the first forest came about. This gathering of a bunch of people was all about showing us how to make a decent joint. The new friend showed us what was needed at least: Weed or hash, leaves, a filter, tobacco and fire. It was the first time for me that i saw real weed there and smelled this scent.

First, he showed us the method of gluing three small leaves into one big one. Then he also showed us large sheets an how to install a filter made from a piece of cardboard. Then the supreme discipline: rolling up. The subject of mixing ratio was also discussed. A really good introduction. Everyone was allowed to take a drag and see how it worked. And we got a really good grin in our cheeks in the process. We laughed together because it was funny to everyone in different ways. And our parents were experiencing us like this is for the first time, but didn´t know what it was all about. Probably the parents thought we just drank too much. Fortunately, the new friend showed us directly a good quality variety. He also told us where to get the stuff. It was not far from the village to the border with the Nederlands. There was also a quite small city park with a stone table in the village. At this stone table met after a few weeks, almost always the same young people. Not only to agree on dates for any parties, but primarily to »smoke« with each other. Smoking here meant not only the normal cigarette. We were a sworn clique.

Through the clique I soon got to know Luke. Luke was the son of parents of Dutch descent. Dutch was spoken at home. Luke had blond hair with a mushroom cut (which was fashionable at the time) and was always dressed cool. Luke once said to me, »You have a black belt in Psycho!« At that time, not only did the Berlin Wall fall, but techno and hiphop music also spilled over to us. The first techno song I knew was »Das Boot« by the group »U96«. The first German hiphop group I knew was »Die fantastischen Vier«. The scene at the stone table established itself more and more as an ordering process for new marihuana from Enschede (Nederlands). Luke and I went on a buying spree with the Walkman almost every weekend. Later we handed the weed over to the people,who ordered it. We tried all kinds of smoking techniques, it was a lot of fun and we had a great time. We found something for our other boredom, which also shot us away in different ways. Luke also became a really good friend along with Keith. We hung out very often together.

I was very often at Luke´s house and we »hung out together«. So we listened to music by »Cypress Hill« or »Limp Bizkit«, smoked pot and drank lots and lots of beer. My school career developed in a very negative way. It wasn`t along before I was onnly pretending to go to school. Instead, sometimes in the morning I secretly bought my first canned beer. For consumption I stayed in inconspicuous places. In former times there was still an old factory area in the village, in which still a couch stood and one could sit down. Of course, I didn´t do that all the time. But rather sometimes here, sometimes there. Also that is was not necessarily noticable. This time with my two best friends was for me retrospectively, the best time in the youth that I experienced. There was still no Internet for the masses. I often stood in front of the front door and drank beer. It was normal for us to be able to visit neighbors when the key was in the door. A key in the door meant »visitors welcome«. You just went in and talked. If you didn´t have a key, you either wanted to be left alone or there was simply no one at home.

Our youngest brother Elias grew tremedously and at some point it was time to move again. And that was to the nearest city, more precisely to a district of it: Allsteppe. As we found out later, the reason was a new pregnancy. And therefore we neede more space, of course. Also meant: another change of school. Again new people and no desire to meet new ones. For me, my friends were those from the village of Schöningen. And not any others. My friends in Schöningen accepted me as I was. No matter whether one had more money or the other a visual impairment. We friends always met on an equal footing. Yes, okay almost always. I even »fought« Keith once in a »fun tournament« on a children´s playground. Which one of us was better at

Ninjutsu or whatever it was called? So we just had our personal fight. Of course, more as a fun and show for those present. Also Keith spontaneously threatened me with his gun several times in his stoner cellar in front of the assembled crew. And I cried with paranoia. I was afraid that a shot might accidentally go off. But afterwards everything was fine again an we went for a walk together. Just as we threw self-made ninja stars at cardboards targets in Rainer´s basement. So for me this school was the last one i attended.

With a leaving certificate of the class 8. In this part of town we lived about one year. When I was on weekend again with Luke, we camped one night at a lake. At night, we took a tour to the next village and then wanted to go back to the tent. But not on foot, we were so tired. Spontaneously and without consultation, I »borrowed« a bike and we rode back. Stupidly, someone saw us. And they reported it to the police. A few weeks later the doorbell rang at home. A man from the district court entered. He asked if I'm really the one that's on his note. He then asked Mom and our stepfather to take a seat to we could talk about »something«. He then said that he had been instructed by the court to initiate an educational measure here. Because I was clearly seen and recognized stealing. I got 25 hours of social work imposed on me. So I had to help a couple of times to hook away the leaves in the cemetery. My first little punishment. Of course momwas not impressed and again dissapointed.

The stepfather started calling me incompetent. I cloud do nothing and would never become anything. I did not care. I had to write this like this. I just wanted to do everything I could to continue to be accepted by my friends. I was just glad that I finally had friends. Until my teenage years, I never felt I had reall friends – except for my cousin. Ever. It just hurt me to move away again from an environment that I finally liked. Where I could just be real. And then it just happened the way it was supposed to happen, without it mattering whether it would be good for me or not. The tone between me and the stepfather became rough.

I didn´t like the new place and the surroundings at all. I always wanted to go back to Schöningen. So I really often hitchhiked back to Schöningen on weekends to visit my friends. With the moped it was a little to far. In the meantime I preferred to listen to music of different directions: Techno, Hardcore or also HipHop. Unusual music attracted me magically. It didn´t take long for hiphop to develop to such an extent that, apart from »Die fantastischen Vier«, American rap music was on everyones lips. But not yet so concisely. I surrounded myself primarily with rap in German: »Aleksey«, »Fettes Brot«, »Samy Deluxe« – that´s what I heard back then. The Album »Lauschgift« was legendary for me.

13. Orientation deficits

A few month later we rally moved to the accociated city: Amaus. The apartment was right on a intersection. Across the street was the municipal library. Next to it was the city police station. I had no plans whatsoever as to what I could become professionally. In order to develop a professional plan, I was registered at a vocational orientation center – BOZ for short. (ger: Berufsorientierungszentrum, eng: Vocational Orientation Center) There were workshops where you could get to know different occupational groups. In a rotation phase, I visited one of the offered work areas for a few weeks. After that, I was able to choose a specific area. I decided on the painting area. I could combine this well with my dreamy thoughts. Certain shapes or objects made me think. The workshop manager came across as very casual with his long hair. His name was John. He liked to listen to music by the group »Red Hot Chili Peppers«. So from then I visited the BOZ an we painted different patterns on wooden boards. From time to time we also practiced putty work.

 Very casual was also my new colleague Johannes. Johannes also opted for the painter´s workshop and listened to slightly different music than I did. He listened to music about darkness, death and other dark themes. So primarily gothic and a lot of hard metal music, where you were sometimes yelled at. Johannes was very diverse when it came to music. So he also brought a CD from the group »Body Count«. Heavy fare for an untrained listener. At that time I used to hitchhike to Schöningen to visit my friends. There was later also in the BOZ the possibility of catching up the high school diploma. So I signed up for it. In addition I also crammed a little. After a few weeks at the BOZ, I met Paul, who lived two towns away, in Bronau. He also liked to smoke his first joint in the park in the morning before work.

I also got along very well with him. There was once an event from BOZ, namely a canoe trip on a river near Münster. The canoe trip as such was phenomenally good. Somethin completly different. As far as that was concerned, the BOZ really had something to offer. Arrived there and briefly set up, we carried the canoes out onto the water. After that we went with the canoes on a river in Munster. It was the Ems or the Werse. And I enjoyed it. Well, in the evening we started drinking beer. With a small group we looked around a little bit in the next village during a walk. Unfortunately there was nothing going on and we walked back. The teamleader John joined us later. He was still at a concert of the rock group »Motörhead«. Later, when I was really drunk, I ran through an nearby cornfield. And grunted like a wild boar. Just embarassing. Then, spontaneously and without prior notice, I sit down in John's beloved VW Bulli. Then I made the buttons down and listened to loud music. I hijacked the van for about 20 minutes. I later surrendered. A little later I had a real blackout. In the morning I woke up and I was sick to my stomach. John made it clear to me by the look on his face that I must have been very stupid. I was angry with myself and ashamed The day ended for me with a bad feeling. The day came at the BOZ when I was allowed to take one of the exams for the secondary school leaving certificate.

Fortunately, before the exam, Paul offered me to do some more to smoke a joint »just quickly« against the exam anxiety. An offer I gladly accepted. So we went to the park just before eight in the morning and he built us a joint. Then we smoked fix the bag and went back relaxed. The intoxication overcame me. The other setting got me down. I was slightly dense at first and walked unobtrusively into the class. We were about eight people and the teacher came in who would test us. That's when things really went downhill physically and in terms of intoxication. The slips of paper were handed out. I was getting warmer and warmer. I looked into the room and everything started started to spin. I couldn't concentrate anymore and was extremely stoned. I got really hot and had chills. My hands and feet started to tingle at the same time. These were the familiar signs of a circulatory collapse. But I also wanted to get the exam done somehow. But: I was ready. Intertwined my hands and rested my head on my arms. I got the unintentionally expected effects and broke out in a sweat.

The teacher noticed that I was not well and came to me.

»Are you not feeling well? Do you want to go outside?«
After I got up, I dragged myself outside sluggishly and
staggering. I had to sit down on the stairs and get som fresh
air. I'm sweating and I couldn't handle it anymore. Then I
saw Paul walking past me, now grinning with glee. »What
an ass« I thought to myself. The teacher came out and
inquired about my condition. I wasn't feeling well at all.
And we agreed that I could make up the exam. I spoke
briefly to one of the social workers at BOZ and then slowly
walked off to see my family doctor. Although the doctor
would have been within a twenty-minute walk, it took me
almost two hours. I had to sit down again and again on the
way because my circulation was causing problems. In
addition to all the consumption, I preferred drinking to
eating and I was very thin. When I arrived, the doctor
measured my pulse and immediately gave me circulatory
drops. After half an hour in the waiting room, where I was
allowed to wait, I felt fit enough to at least walk straight
again. The joint before the exam was not a good idea.
Apart from that, I had problems with minor thefts from
time to time, which were understandably brought up
against me. So very soon I had to do community service
again.

A few days later, as I was dreamily pinning up papers
about new sentences around town, a colleague asked me
why I hadn't turned up for the retest. I idiot forgot the date
for the re-examination. That's why I don't manage to take

the opportunity to get a secondary school diploma here. Once again I had the «idea« that I could improve »a little« here. It was not normal after all. So much for my talents. Another pan before the end of the year in the BOZ. There was in the painting workshop Martin. A blond colleague who was very fond of pranking. Also with him I got along well. Around this time, half-brother Torben saw the light of day. And the »family« continued to grow. It felt very often that we were asked to watch our half-siblings, to give the bottle and to change diapers. Of course I loved my siblings. But I would also have liked to have had more of my own youthful time. After some I used to acknowledge the tasks I took for granted by simply taking off after work on Friday. And I usually didn't come home again until Sunday evening. Of course, the parents didn't like that at all.

At that time, cell phones were only available to very well-off people. I also wanted one because I wanted to be cool. My consumption of alcohol and weed increased massively during this time. It was nothing special for me at sixteen to drink alcohol or smoke pot alone. I tried mushrooms and other chemical drugs for the first time at stoner parties at another friend's house in Schöningen. At that time my musical taste also changed. Instead of normal techno I listened to hardcore and got some »Thunderdome« CDs. The most distinctive music style for me was hip-hop or rap. Favorite groups were »Cypress Hill« or »Wu- Tang Clan«. Both groups were for us simply »Gangster Rap« Groups.

We wanted to be just as cool. Just as much and extreme smoking weed. Making money from things you steal. Make music the same way. But really it was just a desire and a side effect between the ever-increasing consumption. The tendency to consume as much of everything as possible was already developing. And as if by a miracle, Mom soon became pregnant again. And again a move was in the offing. Same city, just a different part of town.

14. Loss of control

After the move to the district of Messum: A few months later, our sister Lucy was born. That brought life into the day. After my time at the BOZ, I thought an apprenticeship as a painter and varnisher might be something for me. The month of August had already begun, so Mom spurred me on to just open the phonebook. I found a painting company where I could start my apprenticeship. And after the first month as an apprentice »pen« (trainee), as if it could have been waited for, I had to pay 400 DM (DM = German Mark, currently round about 200 euro) board money from my salary every month. In the vocational school I met Martin from the BOZ again and was glad that he was there, too. A few months after the start of the training Martin had his birthday and asked me to do the DJ. Of course I gladly accepted.

So my mother drove me to Martin in the afternoon with my stuff. Once there, I set up my setup in the living room. My equipment consisted of a record player – which of course also served as an amplifier. Plus a CD player and relatively normal speaker cabinets. The party was obviously very good. At some point in the morning I just woke up and had a good hangover. When I entered the living room, some of the guests were still sleeping there. The living room lamp was torn down on the floor and otherwise it looked very much like a good party. That confirmed me.

My mother picked me and my stuff up again later.

During this frivolous time, I did something that I regretted for a very long time. There was a weekend when me, Luke and another colleague were out on the town. There came a girl we knew late in the evening. She told us that she wanted to break up with her boyfriend. She said that she was afraid that he would hit her because he was very jealous. We offered to stand by her from a distance in the situation. But in such a way that he did not see us beforehand. She arranged to meet him in a backyard with garages. I was very unhappy with my stepfather and my overall situation at the time and was very vicious in spirit. So that he could not get a chance at all in case he attacked me or anyone, I secretly took a beer bottle with me. This beer bottle had no bottom and I put it in one of my jacket pockets. Back then, I almost always wore parkers because you could fit a lot of things in them. The time to meet came. He came, she came. They met in the middle of the yard and we showed ourselves so that he could see that she had nothing to fear. However, he assessed the situation that we were just going to beat him up. He started a fight with the other colleague after a short back and forth, Luke intervened and it escalated. At that time, he had already drunk quite a bit of alcohol. I went in between as if in a frenzy, pulled the guy to the ground. Then I took the bottle out of my pocket and hit him right in the face. I was intoxicated. It clanked and I let go of him. Luke and the other colleague were confused and taken by surprise by my behavior. They understandably ran away.

The guy had a cut under his eye and was bleeding. I ran away cowardly in the direction of the supermarket. I no longer really understood what I was doing. So I started to question myself, shaking and having problems with my own perception. Is he going to survive? Did I just kill someone? Then suddenly he came running, grabbed me and rammed me into a wall. I begged him, »I'm sorry, I'm sorry, I don't know why I did that either.« He screamed at me, »Because of you I have to go to the hospital now!« Then he let go of me and headed towards the hospital. I was crying and shocked at myself. I didn't know what to do anymore. One hand was full of blood. I myself had a small cut on my hand. I walked around the city without a destination. Later I just sat down in a phone booth and cried. I couldn't just go home like that. I waited for the police. But the police did not come. Maybe he would not press charges and I would get away? I didn't know.

Sometime in the Night a car stopped and a man asked me if he could drive me somewhere. The man drove me home. It must have been about midnight when my mother opened the door for me and let me in. Mom probably noticed that something was wrong, but I couldn't tell. I also hid my hand with the relatively small cut. It was just too violent for me. A few days later I hitchhiked back to Luke and talked to him about it. I was very ashamed. I never thought of myself as being that aggressive. It wasn't long before we were out again that weekend. Both dressed like the last hangmen. We found ourselves in the evening at a stubble field party. There was some GOA so a rather esoteric music. Late at night – we were some kilometers away from Schöningen and Amaus. Then I had the glorious idea to just order a cab for us. I wanted to take Luke home and later trick the cab driver. We called a cab. Brought Luke home. I told the cab driver to drive me to Messum.

Then at a bend – it was still about 500 meters to home – I asked him to pull over to the right. I said I had to get out for a moment, otherwise I wouldn't be able to get my wallet. I got out, then briefly pretended to take out the wallet and ran for it. Just down a street. It was raining a little. He was following me. I overestimated my rusty condition and he actually caught up with me. Then I couldn't take it anymore and surrendered. Then he drove with me to the police. There there was a report and that was it again. I thought. In any case, I got home late at night on foot.

The next day I played the ideal world again at home and felt safe. Then someone drove up in a car. He got out and went to our door. I only noticed that the doorbell rang. The stepfather said »Come on, open up. Let's see who came in«. I went to the door, opened it and looked into the eyes of the cab driver. That's when I got nervous. The cab driver »Oh, look at that. Your father home?« – »Come in!« I heard the stepfather call out. So I had to let the man I »didn't know« in. »Make some coffee!« said the stepfather. And I just made the coffee without comment. The cab driver sat down on the corner bench like a king in a palace and asked, »Is this your boy?« – »Yes, stepson« – »Good to know« – said the cab driver. The stepfather smelled the fuse and asked »Why is something wrong?« That's when the cab driver told our stepfather how we met. After the visit, mom and stepdad really freaked out. I could completely understand in the later years with more maturity. On the other hand, it always seemed to me that the stepfather was primarily concerned only with money.

Our real father wasn't any better either and hadn't paid child support for several months. And so there was soon a court hearing in which I had to testify against my own father. The result was an additional payment of about 1900 DM. The money was transferred to my account. A few days later the money was there and I withdrew money from the ATM. To make it short: There was a lot of noise about money, in which I was certainly not uninvolved. Among other things, I simply went to a country-style disco in the neighboring town. The day after, I woke up at home, confetti was everywhere in the room. Then the door flew open and my stepfather scolded me. I couldn't take it anymore. In the meantime, I often had the desire to just run away. To be able to live my own, self-determined life. I was in my second year of apprenticeship and it was winter.

Probably a not really suitable moment to simply pack the bag. However, I absolutely had to draw a line. Show that a red line has been crossed here. Maybe they also wanted me to move out. At the latest after stepdad's appearance, I felt that way. I just stayed in the room and planned to leave early the next morning. My parents would think I was on my way to work first. I felt terribly sorry for my siblings here because I loved them all. Also for me it was here not easy. But I just had to get out into life at that moment. I just wanted to get away.

15. Up and away

Monday morning. I woke up around 5 p.m., grabbed a sports bag, and packed everything that could be important to me. I put on my jacket and shoes, took the sports bag, and quietly left the house. There was a telephone booth on the street. I went inside and called my boss. I told him that I had been kicked out of my home and wouldn't be able to come to work today. I needed to figure out where I could stay overnight. Although this wasn't true, it felt that way. Mentally, it didn't make a difference to me. This journey from the house to the telephone booth and the conversation with my boss felt like scenes from a movie. The path from Messum to Amaus felt the same way. I was sad that I had chosen this path, but I also had to make that decision. Memories from kindergarten came back to me. Scenes of us leaving our home and moving into the mother-child home. Images of me almost jumping from the second floor. All the anger and sadness that had accumulated over the years resurfaced. The lump in my throat grew bigger, and I cried as I walked. It was emotionally challenging to leave my siblings behind. Yet, I had to change my own situation in order to be happy again. I couldn't do that anymore in my »home«. The meaning and feeling attached to the word »home« had diminished since the separation and dissolution of the family.

I arrived in Amaus and had to walk quite a distance.

Eventually, I hitchhiked to Keith. Keith had no idea about his luck, and I was also afraid that he wouldn't let me in or would tell me to »get lost« or something like that. I walked around him, knocked on his window, and whispered a bit, »Keith!«, »Keith!« – »Yeah, come around« Keith replied. I went to the front door on the other side, and Keith opened it. When I entered his room, I told Keith that I had run away because I couldn't handle my parents anymore. I asked if I could stay with him for a few days until I figured something out. Keith said, »Yes.« Keith even had a bike that he lent me so I could ride the 9 kilometers to work. Then Keith rolled a joint, and I could relax a bit from all the emotional chaos. Later in the afternoon, Keith suggested going to the local youth center to seek help for me. So we went there and explained my situation to the social workers. Unfortunately, they couldn't really help me except for giving me a few tips on who I could reach out to. Suddenly, Mom and my now ex-stepfather showed up in the car, and I saw many yellow bags on the backseat. »Where should we put your clothes?« I thought I hadn't heard correctly.

So it was not only obvious that they wanted me to move out, but they also just put my things in trash bags. Keith saved the situation by saying, »You can put that at my place.« Then they both drove away. Keith and I went back to the farmhouse. When we arrived, I could already see that they had simply left the yellow bags there. It felt like they were just dropping me. Mom and my ex-stepfather were waiting for me there. »Come here,« Mom said. I went over and wanted to know what they had to tell me. »All the child support money you received from your real dad belongs to us, and we would like to have it back, just to make that clear.« I replied, »You're not getting the money back because it was meant for me anyway.« Then I let out another curse word. Well, the latter wasn't necessary, but on the other hand, I just had to let it out.

They drove away and I went to see Keith, who helped me carry my bags in. I was able to put things with Keith for a while. I stayed with Keith so I could just keep working and keep my financial situation at least reasonably stable. But then I realized that I was physically and mentally unable to go to work every day. To cycle the eight to nine kilometers to the painter's booth in the morning and back again in the evening. So I lied to Keith for three days that I was working, even though all the time I was wasting in town was just doing it. I was just lazy and mentally exhausted at the time. On the fourth day, Keith found out I lied to him about my boss calling his house. Of course, that was just crappy of me to my friend. The best friend helped me and instead I just laid back and lazily. So Keith put me in front of the door and said I couldn't stay with him anymore. I could understand that. Keith then gave me a sleeping bag so I wouldn't freeze my ass off outside. I spent a few nights out in the village, sleeping on a bench in the park.

The bench was hidden behind some bushes, so that one was actually relatively well protected in dry weather. So I made my first experiences and slept outside. My aunt's friend also lent me a duffel bag once, in which I could stow a lot of things. In between, I went to Luke's many times. Luke lent me a Walkman and a cassette with the music of »Cypress Hill«. It was mentally as if I had friends in my ear the whole time, who were standing by me in the situation. Nor did it feel like I simply had no roof over my head for a short time. The cold in the night made me however very fast ready. Fortunately I had the sleeping bag from Keith. One night I was allowed to sleep with the former neighbors in the basement. Some times I was also allowed to have breakfast with them. After a few days, I had the idea that I could live on the farm with grandma and grandpa. So I called there and they took me in. An aunt picked me up. I took the rest of the things Keith had left with me. On the farm I shared the room with the younger brother of the Thobass, Reinhard. In the room there was a bed for each of us. Between us a birdcage with a parrot that called around from time to time. The aunt drove me almost every morning with the Ford-Transit to the painter's shop. Or into the city when I had vocational school.

The Ford Transit had problems with the battery in winter. So I had to push the van a few times in frosty temperatures during the winter. Since I couldn't control my alcohol consumption at all at that time, I skipped the vocational school days. I drank beer instead of going to school. Not extremely much. But just like that. Just to switch off. I was 17 and already knew that I was an addict. I realized relatively early on that my drinking behavior was not normal. So I could still remember well that Martin unexpectedly spoke to me in front of the school. He said I should just come back to class with him. So I went along. In the meantime, I dress more and more consciously like a homeless person, e.g. with a parker. When the teacher came in, he asked me if I was even in training. »Well, sure, call!«, I defused the situation. I was busy with my thoughts, with completely different things, like drinking. Shortly before the next break I rolled a cigarette. The teacher walked to the back at that exact moment. So I lit up my cigarette in the front row of the class. So, relaxed in the first row, I lit my cigarette, inhaled a drag and blew the smoke towards the blackboard. »Hey, Jan!!!« whispered Martin to me. »Oh shit!«, I muttered and quickly stomped out the butt. Puffed the smoke as far as possible. The two of us and a few classmates laughed at my somewhat premature smoking break.

On the farm with grandma and grandpa, after a while they also wanted this flat 400 DM board money. I understood that food and drink cost money. But I did not understand why I constantly had the feeling that they were taking too much from me. My aunt and her boyfriend had moved to another village nearby. So I packed my bag and tried to find accommodation with them. But they didn't want that either. And I could understand the situation with one or the other. Who would like to have a third person, who otherwise doesn't have much to do with the family, sitting at home all the time? I set off again for Schöningen.

16. Back to the hometown

It was still winter, and all my moves happened in a very short time. When I arrived in Schöningen, I walked up the hill to Lukas's place. Every time, that long way up. When I arrived, I rang the doorbell, and he let me in. Luke's parents were probably not always pleased with my spontaneous visits in an unusual appearance. So, I soon got used to quietly knocking on Luke's or Keith's window instead of ringing loudly, also because I felt ashamed. Luke, like Keith, was a true friend who always treated me well. For example, Luke often gave me fresh clothes to wear, so I could freshen up. I also sought help from social services. I explained my situation clearly and said that I couldn't get along with my stepfather anymore and needed a place to live, also so I could continue working. But I was told »Since you have the option to return home but choose not to, we unfortunately cannot help you.« Well, thanks for nothing.

I couldn't avoid it and had to drop out of my apprenticeship. In the last six months, I almost exclusively painted radiators with flood paint. After that, I always felt a bit lightheaded. When I applied for unemployment benefits at the job center, I mentioned that this work also gave me constant headaches, so I couldn't continue doing it. A few days later, I celebrated my eighteenth birthday. I still remember how I gifted myself a Walkman for my birthday. I often commuted between Luke and Keith to avoid bothering either of them for too long. By now, I had gotten used to sleeping outside. But it wasn't summer; it was very, very cold. Back then, at the soccer field further down in Schöningen, on a field a few meters away from the path, there was a thick tree trunk. I would hide behind it at night to sleep.

There I lay behind it and usually rolled myself a cigarette before falling asleep. With one sleeping bag, it was quite manageable here or in the barn a few meters away, as long as it wasn't too cold. One of the best moments was the following one. On New Year's Eve, when everyone had a home and was with their families, there was a friend here who thought of me. Luke walked down at night – from his home high up on the hill, down to the soccer field by my tree trunk, woke me up, and said, »Happy New Year!« He also handed me a joint. I will never forget that gesture. A friend who cared about how I was doing and showed that he was there for me. Just like Keith, he showed me that he was a true friend. I knocked on both of their windows so many times, and they always helped me as best they could.

As the temperatures outside were quite low, it eventually happened as it had to. I got pneumonia and felt like I could only breathe half of the time. It became very, very difficult, and I presented myself to a doctor in the village. There, they simply gave me something to inhale. But it only improved to a certain extent because I was still sleeping outside. So, I sought advice from our former neighbors.

Rainer's mother suggested that I simply call my father. That could indeed be the solution and offer me a kind of fresh start. Well, at least supposedly. To be completely, completely honest: I was already very, very addicted back then. I was also caught stealing several times in the supermarket in Amaus.

But I didn't care. As long as I drank beer or alcohol, I just didn't care. I already knew that addiction was increasingly taking over my daily life, or I planned my daily routine to consume as much alcohol or other drugs as possible. Well then, I called my father and asked him if he could pick me up. After all, I could barely breathe anymore and had no other place to stay at that point. He was living in Brokolt at the time, on the first floor of his grandmother's apartment. The neighbors used to live there before. Grandma still lived on the second floor. Upstairs, there was another room where my father had his bedroom. On the ground floor, there was a guest room. I could stay in there. It was a huge relief that my father came to pick me up. I recovered in the warm apartment after a few days and started feeling better. My relationship with my father still wasn't easy, though. However, during this phase of addiction, he and my grandma trusted me. On the other hand, I was losing control more and more often and consumed way too much. I started receiving unemployment benefits again.

Without my father's knowledge, I obtained a credit card from a bank that was heavily advertised on television. To my surprise, as an unemployed person, I was actually sent a real credit card. After being assigned a job as a wallpaper remover through the job center, I found myself increasingly drawn to the bus station during my free weeks. This place from my childhood had a magical pull on me once again. The homeless people were talkative and shared their stories while drinking. From the station, you could take a bus directly to the Netherlands. I also boarded a few times and crossed over. In the Netherlands, I bought some weed and returned on the bus while being high. I met David at the station and got along well with him. It wasn't far from my apartment to his place, so I started going to his place more often than the bus station. We consumed quite often in his apartment. He also knew Torte, a punk who had an apartment a few streets away in the rough neighborhood. A girl from the neighborhood, who occasionally smoked weed, befriended a man, likely a Romanian. It didn't take long for them to become a couple.

The Romanian was also visiting the Torte from time to time and soon I found out why. He asked me one day if I would be willing to register cars in my name. There would be for it also a few euros. For each car so 350 € on the hand. Directly after the registration. Since I could use the money of course for consumption well, I registered ten cars in my name in one week. I did not see the costs that would arise for me, but simply the money at that moment. So in a very short time I spent all the money on alcohol and drugs and regularly catapulted myself into a film tear. One day when I was back at the bus station, I wanted to withdraw money from the account. I found out through a test that I could overdraw the account. So I went and withdrew as much money as I could every day. I overdid it a lot with consumption during that time and also drank way too much alcohol. My father began to worry.

 One December 22, I went to town in the afternoon to broaden my horizons, and bought three blotters. So-called »Pappen«, i.e. square pieces of cardboard, which contained LSD. The symbol printed on them were ice cream waffles. At home, I divided one of them into four equal-sized pieces. Based on my previous experience, I didn't want to overdo it here, of course. At least not right away. So I went out for a bit and came back late in the evening. Downstairs in the apartment I was allowed to use, there was a living room and a kitchen. The kitchen had been converted by my father into a sort of computer workstation. In the living room was an older but wellpreserved sofa set. This consisted of a two-seater and a three-seater. And a normal armchair. In the living room was also a small music system, with which one could play CDs. So I took two of the small pieces of cardboard and played a racing game on the PC. After about 30 minutes I was driving pretty fast and noticed how my hands were getting quite warm. I finished the game and turned off the PC. From then on, I clearly felt the muscles in my jaw area tense up and I just started to get really excited. So I got up and took the other two pieces. Thus I had a complete piece intus. I stood at the stereo and looked over to the kitchen and saw half the computer table from there. Suddenly, I saw the table disappear into the room to the left. I could not believe my eyes. I had never experienced anything like that before. Then I knew that »those things« were starting to work. At the music system I put in a »Happy Rave« CD.

The music system gave its best and I started to dance. After about three hours, I took another piece. Effortlessly I danced full of joy and without worries, into the early morning. It was around ten o'clock when I longed to slow down a bit. But I couldn't. I had to grin constantly and had an extreme urge to move. So I made a plan to hitchhike to Amaus, where we once lived. One of my aunts lived there with her boyfriend, who knew about my consumption. They could possibly help me. So I just hitchhiked and arrived about three hours later. I had no real sense of time anymore. Because it was: Christmas Eve. After a few hours at my aunt's, I finally got off Trip. I would have liked to spend the night with them, but they didn't want that. So I called my father (who didn't even know I was there) and asked that he please pick me up. Of course, my father wasn't impressed at all, but of course he picked me up anyway. I apologized for the action and so we celebrated Christmas Eve after all. In the new year, I felt lost in addiction. One night I secretly took Dad's car keys to

David and with a other colleagues we went to the garage, some ways away from the apartment. To give my colleague David something to make money again, I gave him the fishing rods from my father. We took the car and David's colleague then drove us around. Meanwhile we listened to music from the »Spice Girls«. Another moment I would never forget. We returned the car undamaged later. The next morning, Grandma rang David's doorbell and asked for me. She was obviously worried and a little angry. She asked what we had done and that I should come home to apologize to Dad. I said I would come back later. Later I went back and of course I cashed in extreme anger for my behavior. I told my father that I had to give money to my colleagues so that I could somehow justify myself. During the stages of addiction, of course, I lied. I certainly wasn't just the victim. I hurt people who liked and loved me in my »wet phase«. It is what it is. The main thing was that I could continue to somehow finance my consumption.

Then a few days later, David and I were supposed to watch over the apartment of the punk Torte. Torte had to make a statement to the police. He still had weed hidden in his couch and suspected that guys might show up on the same day. Who probably knew from his stupidity that there was something else hidden in the couch. They knew he had more, because they bought weed from him before. And then it became afternoon and the nice colleagues showed up. I'd had a few beers in the meantime and stood in front of the front door »You don't even have to fool around here. You could just go!« Then one of them asked me. »What do you want, you half shirt?« That provoked me of course, the anger from the school time came up. And in this neighborhood, you don't let anyone tell you anything. I went straight at him and wanted to impress him. There he went a piece to the side and I was still surprised when I suddenly fell to the ground. Another colleague had secretly climbed onto the garage roof from behind and jumped into my back. I lay on the floor and received several kicks to my face and body. David stayed in the apartment by the window. The guys finally made their way and I scrambled to my feet.

 I went back to the apartment and tended to my aches and pains. I lost a molar tooth in the process. Still, we kept our word and didn't let anyone into the apartment. I calmed down and continued drinking beer. By the way, there was a stolen car from the Romanian colleague outside. Actually, Torte was supposed to take care of the car. Later we got bored. Torte did not come back at all. We hid the grass well and drank some more. David and I often looked at the car key and then we looked at each other questioningly. So we decided to grab the car and he drove off with us. I was allowed to make a few attempts in the parking lot, but I couldn't drive a car yet, so he just drove on. Then suddenly my light went out.

 I woke up and felt severe pain in my left arm. I screamed.

They tried to calm me down »You had a car accident and are about to have surgery.« I asked, »Where is my colleague David?« »He's already in surgery. He'll be fine.« My eyes fell shut again. When I woke up, I was told that we had crashed into a tree on an avenue at just under 100 km/h. We were both very lucky to survive that. I had a left humerus fracture (splinter fracture) and a concussion. They put a splint in my upper left arm and screwed the element in place with two screws at the top of the joint. David had a broken jaw, a fracture in his left leg and also a concussion. After a week, I was allowed to go home again. Another week later David was also back home and sitting on his much loved couch again. Leg in plaster and a strange harness around his jaw. At least he could talk, grin dirty and eat on his own. David was always good for surprises.

So he showed me a big salad bowl full of magic mushrooms, so-called »Magic Mushrooms«. That's when my eyes started to light up. He just reached into the bowl, gave me the handful and said, »Here – eat!« We listened to cool house music and he invited a few more people to join him. The effect of the mushrooms was not long in coming. I saw many colors right in the middle of the room and clouds flying. Objects were partially distorted and my own self spoke to me. Suddenly the doorbell rang. And he asked me to let the girls in. I was disturbed. Why were girls coming now? I was not prepared for that and became restless. David lived on the second floor. I went to the door rather uncertainly and pressed the button for the door opener. That is, the mechanism with which you could open a door downstairs from a distance. I was still standing upstairs and looking down the stairs. The girls were so incredibly pretty to me at that moment that I couldn't believe it.

Were they really that pretty or was I imagining it? I walked irritated back to the room. David noticed my nervousness and simply said, »Sit down, boy! Relax!« The girls came in and I got very, very nervous. I hadn't really eaten much that day either. Now my circulation was throwing a wrench in the works. I felt my feet start to tingle. I knew then that this was not a good sign. The tingling now started in my hands as well and I fainted without any other sign. When I woke up again, I was lying on the floor and those present were worried about me. »Come up, all is well!« they said, and »Here is a glass of water.« So I found myself sitting in the round, me with my glass of water. Breakfast is important.

17. Mark the big Max

Back home in the apartment with dad and grandma. At some point, the many letters from the insurance companies piled up and my father asked me about it. I opened up and told him what it was all about. He then helped me to deregister all the cars again. So he drove off with me all the insurance and we were able to cancel most of the policies. For the most part, the insurance companies were gracious and understood the connection to the addiction. As a prerequisite, however, they demanded that I go to the police and report myself. And that's what I did. Because the many, many bills that fluttered into the house were not few. The vehicles were used to commit crimes or to run »various errands«. But I also knew that if I made the statement to the police, the colleagues would no longer belong to my circle of friends. They would much rather go on "a trip" with me. I had to exaggerate constantly. I was no longer surprised that after the following action, my dad could no longer develop any motivation to further support my misconduct.

Days later, I went back to the bus station and got drunk again. Later that afternoon, an ex-con showed up at the bus station pretending he had to mark »big Max« there. At the time I didn't give a shit about much, very much. In any case, later I had another film tear and got into it with the guy. The police took me into custody and I woke up in the morning in a drunk tank. Then the policeman gave me the friendly hint that my father brought me some spare clothes. Because the other clothes were no longer usable. In a film tear I completely lost control over my mind and body. But then a policeman told me further »By the way, you should not show up at your father's anymore. He doesn't want to see you anymore.« I could understand that. So I put on what I could and walked back to the bus station. Once there, one of the homeless people told me what I had done. The guy I had messed with had been in prison for several years. Because he almost bled a person dry with a knife in his apartment. The person just barely survived. But that also means that I must have had a lot of luck. I should be told not to show my face at the station. The guy would be really mad at me. So I looked far away.

After the optional meeting place bus station became taboo for me, I went to David. Then another colleague came to visit and we thought about how we could shoot each other down again. Then the friend said we could come with to his home. His parents would be gone and we could get from the father a »little« of his home-distilled liquor. The good friend lived in a high-rise building on about the fifth or sixth floor.But fortunately there was an elevator. No sooner said than done. We sat in the living room. The colleague walked through the apartment and came back with a white plastic gallon. One glass for each of us. He filled my glass to a little more than half. I smelled it and the most appropriate note would be: methylated spirits. The good stuff was supposed to be over 70% alcohol. I just downed the stuff in two big gulps. And that, although it tasted really bad. The colleague gave me half a glass again, which I also emptied quickly. I still felt briefly how the warmth from the legs pulled up to my head and then it became dark.

My head felt very, very heavy. It felt like it was about to burst. Then I realized that I was in the hospital. To my left was a whole bunch of devices showing different things. My goodness, I felt sick. As soon as I was awake, an orderly came into the aquarium with a bowl »Here. Wash yourself, you look like shit.« He added a washcloth and a towel and left again. I was only dressed with a thin cloth around my body. Down beside the bed a bag, with my clothes. Plus a couple of empty wine bottles. Something really bad must have happened. The doctor later told me that I also had a head injury that I hadn't noticed until now. Then I felt the bump on the back of my head. There was an emergency call: an unconscious person was in the elevator of a high-rise building. In the basement. When the first responders arrived, they found me unconscious and naked. So they pulled me out of the elevator completely naked and put me in the ambulance to be treated. I was so sick that I didn't feel halfway normal until the second day. I had severe alcohol poisoning. On top of that, I had a bruise between my brain and the top of my skull. That's when I started to panic and fear for my life. To check whether the bruise was receding, I was taken to a hospital in the city Bochum. There they x-rayed my head. Fortunately, the bruise had receded. I just wanted to leave Brokolt. So I called mom and asked if I could live with them again. At least until I had a job and an apartment again. Luckily they picked me up the day I was released and drove me back to their apartment in Amaus.

18. Magic Mushrooms

After Mom and Stepdad got me out of Brokolt, I was happy as punch to finally get some rest. My plan was to at least slow myself down a bit from the consumption level. Or to start from scratch, at least the thought occurred to me every now and then. On the second day, I visited my aunt and her boyfriend. I always got along well with them. One day later I hitchhiked to Schöningen again. I got some beer cans, packed them in a tote bag and went to the park to the stone table. But there was nobody there. I went on to the school, which bordered directly on the park. In fact, I run into two good colleagues there. Both of them were sitting there quite stoned and looked at me completely aghast. I finally came after a very long time simply around the corner and said »Moin!« – »Where does he come from?« one colleague asked the other. »I'll be back more often now« I said and started drinking my beer. Of course, it didn't stop with just one can. Later, Luke joined us and he was happy that I was back »at the start«.

Later, back in the apartment with Mom, everything was okay at first. I thought. But I noticed that the atmosphere was somehow strange. In fact, the question came from the stepfather »What about board money? Because you can't live here for free.« Then I got a really, really thick lump in my throat. I asked »Really? Is it always about the money? I'm just here and bang, I'm supposed to pay money again? I don't even have a job yet!« In the meantime, I met enough people who simply share instead of just taking. I got angry, packed my bag and just walked out. Mom called down something from the balcony above, which I did not understand and did not want to understand. I kicked over another pile of yellow bags (bags with plastic garbage for recycling process) outside and cursed. I went to my aunt and her boyfriend. There I could come almost any time, because both knew the family problems. Once there, I told them what happened and said I didn't know what to do.

Then the friend told me that the two would soon move. And I could have the apartment as a next tenant. Thus I would only need a job and the problem would be solved. A few weeks later, I was sitting in this little attic flat. On top of that, the uncle got me a job through a temp agency. The car accident had been about a year ago at that point. I started working for a company that made pliers. I had neither the talent nor the skill for that. I regularly had metal splinters in my fingers. The subsequent work assignment was more pleasant. I worked in a Dutch company and mounted strips on wooden panels. The company provided Wooden elements. Elements in the form of panels, with which you could quite easily, separate or divide premises. A week later I was able to work in another area. Now I was supposed to insert wooden panels into a machine.

After I had inserted some boards into the machine together with another employee, I felt a crack in my left shoulder. I felt on the left side that the screws had loosened. It hurt and I informed the foreman. After work, I was instructed to have my shoulder checked by the family doctor. The family doctor gave me a referral to the hospital, where the splint would be surgically removed. So I packed a bag at home and went to the hospital. However, the pressure of addiction was getting to me again. Even at this time with a job and work, it was unfortunately »normal« for me to drink after work. On the second day in the hospital, I had an operation under general anesthesia to remove the splint and the screws. I was in a four-bed room with three patients. One bed was still unoccupied. On the third day, funnily enough, an acquaintance became my new instep man. Some kind of pain. No idea what he had exactly. As boring as the day started, I didn't want this one to end. I got dressed as if I would be outside a Round walk and went downstairs. Downstairs I just got into a cab and went »just to Holland«. Went to a store in Enschede, bought »magic mushrooms« and had them drive me back. Yes, the cab fare was more expensive than the mushrooms. But at least I had something to get my teeth into. When I got to the room, I went to the bathroom and put a portion aside for my colleague.

Then I came back out and handed him his portion during a smoke break on the balcony. After lunch, we agreed to take the mushrooms after supper. It could be that I still love to eat mushrooms today because of the taste. As soon as we finished dinner, he and I ate some mushrooms. And then I just fell asleep. When I woke up, I saw my bed neighbor moving rhythmically to the music from the TV. As if he were dancing. He looked over at me with a grin and I noticed that I perceived everything much more colorfully than would normally be the case in reality. One of the fellow patients looked over a little worried. He didn't really know what to make of the situation. I was also cheerful and happy about this moment and went to the terrace with my colleague. We smoked normal cigarettes and it really felt like being on vacation. We saw the sunset in the distance and it just felt carefree good. No pain in the arm. The My colleague also had no more pain and said later in the room »So! I have no more pain now. I'm leaving now!« So I said »No problem, see you around.« The colleague did indeed leave.

When the colleague was gone, I lay in bed and worried. I shouldn't have done that. I had a photo of my siblings on the nightstand by the bed and was staring at it. Then, in the midst of a trip on mushrooms, I realized what I had already done wrong. I got a terribly sad movie and started crying. I had no idea how to describe this emotional twist, but mushrooms show you what it looks like deep inside. I mumbled in my sad state that I missed my siblings and that I had already done a lot wrong and so on. So this lousy movie went on for a really long time. I cried for two hours without end. A bed neighbor from opposite could not stand it and comforted me. I later apologized for my behavior. I was just glad that no one called in one of the nurses. I probably would have been admitted to psychiatry. Sometime later I finally fell asleep. The next morning: when I woke up, I had a huge head and felt completely burned out. The act of sadness was taking its toll. Before rounds even started, I went to the bathroom and washed my face several times with cool water. When I came out of the bathroom, I once again thank the rest of the bedfellows. That day I just stayed relaxed and rehabilitated myself.

Two days later I was finally discharged. One week later. I was standing at the stove and my food was sizzling in the pan when the front doorbell rang. I did not manage to give the company a yellow slip (notice of illness). Now came the receipt. I opened and looked into the face of the head of the temp agency. He began a monologue about my progress in the company so far, when he suddenly remarked »Your food is on fire.« I was mentally still with his story and overheard that. He »Your food is on fire!« – »Oh shit«, there was actually already a lot of smoke over the stove. Burnt. Kind of like »my work relationship«. As I walked back to the door, he noted that I was no longer employed by the temp agency. That was it. Honestly, it was my own fault. But in the recklessness of addiction, it just didn't matter. I was just too used to sleeping outside. Something like that couldn't shock me anymore. In truth, this was the addict talking out of my head. The main thing is to drink! Doesn't matter shit. So I signed up for unemployment again under some pretext and spent my time again doing what I did best: listening to »Cypress Hill« and boozing.

One day, while I was sitting in the park, a guy with Turkish roots came by who said we could just make money and then consume something. I hitchhiked with him to Bronau. There he fetched a car radio from some other colleague. With it we went to a run-down accommodation, which he shared with another. We watched Turkish television but I could only guess at the content. He shared his food with me. There were peppers, tomatoes, hot peppers and bread. Later we hitchhiked back to Amaus and there to a dealer. He went in alone and exchanged the radio to »browns« that is stretched heroin. With that we went to my apartment on the top floor. Here we smoked the stuff on an aluminum sheet. You never forget that smell. Immediately after inhaling, the turn came. I could feel my pulse slowing down and getting warm. The drying of the glasses slowed down immensely and only happened in slow motion. The insidious thing about the drug is that it feels so good. It's like a warming blanket that they put on you. You don't feel any pain anymore. We drank tea and smoked the stuff away.

Later, the colleague said goodbye and left.

19. Hard on it

I went to the supermarket pretty much every day, got some beer, sat down on one of the seats at the bus stop and drank. At that time, this bus stop had orange seats. And I drank one beer after another. One morning I woke up at home with a big hangover. I didn't know how I had made it home. There were wrapped packages of sausages on the kitchen counter. But ones where you usually cut the sausage into slices. Normally these are always behind the pane. I must have stolen these. But how did I get this out unnoticed? So I carefully went to the K+K and thought about how I could find out. I went in and just bought a can of beer. Whatever else. But nothing happened. So I had nothing to worry about. Another day at the bus stop: I was standing there already pretty drunk and talking to myself when a girl came up to me and said »What are you doing here every day? You don't look like a homeless person.« I said »I'm not homeless, I just prefer being outside to being inside.« Then she said, »But drinking so much beer isn't healthy either, is it? Shall I take you home? Wait, I'll get some friends of mine.« »Okay« I said. And then I continued to drink beer. In fact, she left and came back about 20 minutes later with four other girls. And they started interviewing me »Hi, where do you live?« and »Can you show us where you live?« The chatter between the girls started and I said, also to cut it short »Okay, okay we'll just go to my pad now.«

But then I was already not quite as fit and so the girls supported me a little while running. The small flat was also not very far away. Arrived there, I sat down on my sofa bed in the sparsely furnished room. The girls sat down makeshift on the floor. I had only the small kitchen with an equally small counter. Next to it a small TV on a small table. There the girls talked away. Like exorcists who would try to banish the addiction to alcohol from my soul. At some point I said, »Sorry but I'm just tired.« And took off my sweater. I was so tired that I just eventually fell asleep. When I woke up, I looked around. There were over twenty yellow sticky notes labeled and scattered around the apartment. »Stay dry!«, »We believe in you«, »Don't drink!« and similar appeals were written down. I asked myself »What should I do with such notes?« And I went back to K+K and got two cans of beer to wake up. By the way, I didn't see the girls again. What a pity. Maybe in my drunkenness I only saw the ones I wanted to see.

20. First attempt at therapy

This phase of preferring to be outside was strange. I realized that I was completely at the mercy of the addiction. I had lost my job. The perspective became bleak and I found myself very deep in my victim role again. Then there was this day where I was extremely drunk again at the supermarket listening to »Cypress Hill«. A man came up to me whom I had seen several times. He said »You don't belong here. You have a neat appearance and I know that you are struggling with the alcohol inside. What if I showed you how to get out of it?« So I said »I have another problem right now. I locked myself out of my home and lost my keys.« That's when he said, »It's not a problem, believe me. If you say I don't feel like it anymore, then come with me.« I simply accepted the offer and went with him. The man lived not far away in the city, together with his wife. He explained to me how it worked that people got »clean«. First, one would come to the hospital, as a precursor to proper detoxification in a clinic. From there, he said, you could then be referred and do therapy. The man also offered to get my clothes from my apartment so I wouldn't have to go home again, but could go directly to the hospital.

So I found myself at the hospital in the afternoon. The man even fetched the things from my loft. By the way, he kicked the door in for that, which I thought was very cool.

I finally had the feeling that there were people who really cared about me and gave me the feeling that I was worth something. I was in the hospital for a week and they arranged a detox place for me in a clinic in Munster. When my mom heard about it, she even drove me there. On the way to the right building, I saw another house of the clinic, on it there was a kind of closed exit. But in this enclosure there were no animals, but people with obvious mental disabilities. It looked to me like some kind of exit. A small group of people were walking around in it, seemingly without any apparent purpose. One of these people looked at me. This look was very, very empty and yet questioning. Traumatizing in the truest sense of the word.

Arriving at the »Lighthouse« detoxification center building, a group of patients were returning from a walk. I said goodbye to mom. One of the girls asked somewhat teasingly, »What are you doing here?«. I said »Detoxify.« Then came the answer »Detox? This is where you get the hang of it.« I left the answer as it was. I could not classify this answer due to lack of experience. I saw for the first time a detox clinic from the inside for the first time. I hadn't expected to meet people from such different backgrounds. What did I notice? There were really pretty women here who didn't look like they had taken hard drugs. What you quickly noticed here was that everyone here was the same. They all had negative backgrounds and were here trying to get out. Some were given medication, others were not. I was given a drug as a precaution to prevent withdrawal symptoms. I had already become acquainted with withdrawal symptoms. If I drank excessive amounts of alcohol the day before and woke up in the morning, my body would shake violently. It was as if the right side of my stomach was contracting. It really contracted. Usually the body relaxed only after two cans of beer. And with beer cans I got if, generally half liter cans. Now back to my career. I got the chance for a therapy in a specialized clinic. I accepted the chance and it didn't take long before a person from community service picked me up and drove me there. After an initial medical examination, we started with lunch, where I was introduced by name. So everyone knew my name immediately and knew what I looked like. After that, one of the clients took me under his wing and showed me the building, which consisted of several residential units. After that I moved into a two-bed room and it continued with the instruction on the house and therapy rules.

 The therapy concept was strict but fair. The daily program was to the minute but structured. In the discussion round, which took place every morning, the conditions were queried and current topics were addressed directly. Here, none of the clients could hide. One was not allowed to lean against the wall. The clients were all extreme people. Interesting how people of different cultures had to get along here. Everyone was so different. I also learned the

Turkish game here »Okey« know. Something similar to »Rummikub«. There was now and then also a lot of conflict potential. Here some showed their true colors. The therapists could quickly see through seemingly tough people. Often the criminal energy was still very deeply anchored. Clients were also downright addicted to constantly tricking each other. The cleverer the trick, the more attention there was. And there were the classic rule breakers. It took a few weeks before I was caught, too.

The infraction: secretly smoking in the backyard with another client. In this facility, this was a serious violation of the rules, which resulted in immediate dismissal from therapy. I had to pack my things and leave immediately. I took the train to Portmund. There I was something a week on the road. The temperatures were relatively cool, but still just about bearable. Again I heard music of »Cypress Hill« over my Walkman. I got me hash, because it also from the effect but also from the taste always preferred. Official places to sleep for the homeless were usually out of the question for me, since the people there often complained to each other. Instead, I preferred to sleep in savings banks next to a bank statement printer or corners of an underground parking garage. Often I simply searched for meaning and believed in karma. And didn't want to get on the nerves of any of my relatives or acquaintances. Instead, I »studied« people in the wild.

After a little over a week I was simply through and

hitchhiked back to Amaus. So I found myself again at the K+K. With a bag full of clothes. No more apartment and no more job. A long, long time began. I often hitchhiked back to Luke or Keith. I hung out in the park at Schöningen very often in phases. For almost a year I was in Amaus at K+K every day. On warmer days I did my laundry at my aunt's and hung the still damp clothes out to dry at the bus stop. Quite dull. Was certainly strange for some people, but I also had to get my laundry dry somehow. Sometimes there was no alternative. Sometimes I just slept at the bus stop. Woke up and saw that one had put a few cigarettes on the seat next to me. Or a bit of change. In the morning, there were schoolchildren who simply pressed their food into my hand. I saw what others only knew from the media. To get money for beer, I stole cigarettes and sold them in front of the supermarket. Then I would go back in and buy beer. And the whole thing several times a day.

I saw the other side of the system. People who drove or walked to work every day. I also found it rebellious to just abuse the system. Because it didn't help me in those phases either. Well, not always. If you didn't have an apartment, you didn't get a job. For those who always had an apartment, it was easy to just complain. In the summertime, I lay on the green meadow by the cemetery, where no one really disturbed me. There were also phases in between where I managed not to drink in the morning. Or sometimes not for the whole day. But these were quite rare. But to detoxify myself now and then, I did. I withdrew myself from the scene and stayed a bit away from people. There where no one shows up. Searched for better places to sleep, simply to not always have to walk such long distances. Process optimization on the plate. That was not always easy with a duffel bag.

21. Hitchhiking

When I needed a new pair of pants, I would »get« one from the rack outside a store. This saved me the cramp of getting it back out. I listened to »Cypress Hill« almost daily on Luke's incredibly energy efficient Walkman. The thing really only needed one battery and it lasted what felt like forever. Once I was so incredibly pissed off about my situation at K+K that I threw a half-full beer can in a high arc towards the park at a late hour. Every day the same situation. I woke up, went to the K+K, looked at the people, drank beer, smoked cigarettes. Every now and then I would just smoke a joint. If I had weed or hash. Just like that. In the middle of the day. Nobody cared. At the old train station there was an empty house on the left side. There Luke and I smoked weed secretly a few times. At the top there was another attic, but it was full of junk. Here I made a path to the very back. In the back there was another small elevation and another area that was dry. Buddy Johannes, whom I still knew from BOZ times, gave me blankets and helped me to make a relatively good sleeping place here.

 Here I slept almost every night and for over a year. I had a mattress and an old wardrobe, which we turned into a shelf. There we made a curtain out of fabric. So that I had a kind of supply shelf. The only drawback was the noise of the young people who celebrated their parties downstairs in the youth club. But that was only the smallest evil. In between, I had to go to a German Armed Forces office one day for muster. Just as a side note. One sunny day on the weekend, Luke and I hitchhiked to Munster. We wanted to pick up a few girls. There were then also two, which we approached. To have some peace and warmth, it was a bit chilly outside at the time, we went into a church. After we went out, the one girl wanted my jacket because it was so cold. The way I was taught, you help each other and so I gave her my jacket. Even though I was homeless. Luke said »Jan! She's pulling you off!« I still meant very confidently »No, not an issue.« Then the two said they had to go away for a short time and would be right back. There I meant still quite credulous »Okay, see you soon.« Both girls then went up the street and turned left. Of course they did not come back and I stood there: without jacket.

Then, a day later, back in Amaus, I was at my uncle and aunt's house. There, drunk, I cut my identity card with a pair of scissors. And so the next day I was standing at the K+K with only what I was wearing. This recurring days when I allowed myself to get drunk again were like a never-ending story. Like something out of a movie. A new day. I left my things in my accommodation at the station, and walked around a little. At a traffic circle in the direction of the Netherlands, a colleague stood and hitchhiked. »Hey do you want to come? Wanted to go over and smoke a little.« »Sure« I said, and we hitched first to a town before the border and then over to the Netherlands. I guess he knew a coffee shop that I was unfamiliar with until then. As usual, I had already had a few beers and we arrived. You could only enter the coffeeshop if you made it up the steel stairs to the second floor.

He invited me and the store had what felt like a club atmosphere and we smoked pot. The new setting affected my circulation. I told him that I needed to get some fresh air outside the door. I walked very slowly down the stairs, holding onto the banister. Fear of heights set in. Not really my thing, I thought. My circulation was really getting me down again. Finally I reached the bottom and sat down. I couldn't bring myself to want to make my way back up. My colleague was still up there. And I was down here and didn't know what to do. So I decided to just hitchhike back to town myself. But I couldn't remember exactly where I was! I walked a few streets further and found myself on a main road. Where, drunk and disorientated, I asked Dutch people how I could go to Germany. But I could hardly keep on my feet and the sense of time was gone.

I saw the logo of the Dutch police in the corner of my eye and my eyes went black. When I woke up, I suddenly found myself in a prison cell. »Oh, my God« I thought. »What had I done now?« A sandwich and a packet of milk were handed through a flap in the door. When they opened the door, I asked what had happened. One of the policemen said that I had simply been taken into custody so that I wouldn't run in front of a car while drunk. So I thought »Phew, I was really lucky again.« I was looking forward to being able to hitchhike in the direction of Amaus, strengthened and free.

22. Surprise

Then I asked »Okay, then I can go now, right?« But then the policewoman said surprisingly »No, you still owe seventy guilders in the Netherlands.« (Currency of the Netherlands just before the introduction of the Euro). She went on to say, »You have two choices. Either you can pay the money or call someone to pay it. If you can't pay the money, you will have to spend a week in a Dutch jail.« My jaw dropped at that point. I asked, »Where did this amount come from?«

»Once a car was parked in the wrong place, you were the owner, and this resulted in penalties, which are still outstanding.« Then it occurred to me: These were still liabilities from the cars registered at that time, with which the persons were also on the road in the Netherlands. All right. Who should I call? Of course, I dialed the number of the person I thought could and wanted to save my situation: my mom. So I bravely and confidently picked up the phone and dialed mom's number. Mom picked up and listened to me. I asked her to lend me the seventy guilders and also told her that otherwise I would have to spend a week in prison. »Yes, boy, you'll have to deal with that yourself. I can't give you anything.« That was the end of the phone call. Ouch. I announced meekly that unfortunately could not raise the money. So I was allowed to get into a van a few minutes later and we drove towards Groningen.

The radio was playing »Wild, Wild West« by Will Smith. A moment that burned itself in. The stay began with bad fears. When I came in, I had to undress completely and go straight to the shower. I thought that was it. Now I'm going to get a real rough ride. So I was led to a cell for four people. I didn't know anyone there. In the morning, a judicial officer always came and distributed the medication to the inmates. The toilet was only connected to the cell by a flap door. So you could hear and smell everything when you went to the toilet. I was also afraid that I would now have to »build a bus«. What this means is that you cover the underside of a bed with blankets and then do a service to one of the prisoners. Fortunately, I was spared that. Instead, I had to scrape the aluminum lid off a yogurt pot clean. So that we could smoke heroin.

After a week I was finally allowed to leave for Germany. They even gave me money for a train ticket to Germany. And the tip not to let the authorities check me on the way. Because if I didn't have the seventy guilders with me again, there would be a repeat. So off I went, bought myself at the station a Ticket and drove off. In Zwolle I had to change trains once. So I got off in Zwolle (half of the route) and walked around the station. Just before the next train towards Germany arrived, I noticed that I no longer had the ticket in my pocket. I must have lost it somewhere around here. So I walked restlessly around the station and looked to see if the ticket was lying somewhere there. But it wasn't lying anywhere. It was simply gone. Now I also became a fare dodger unintentionally. The train came, I got on and promptly grabbed a large Dutch newspaper. I sat down and just pretended to read it. Hopefully this trip will go without a check, I hoped. Then the door opened and a ticket inspector walks past me towards the next car. Obviously he asked if anyone had boarded. To which I promptly replied with the most Dutch-sounding »Nee« possible. And fortunately for me, he just kept walking.

Eventually the train arrived in Germany and I was so happy. My destination was, of course, the familiar bus stop in Amaus, where I rested. What a week.

23. Two weeks correctional facility & Court date

For a long time, the new identity card contained the note »without fixed abode«. The court date for the assault was still pending. Therefore, I had to present myself at least once a week to the local police. So that they knew that I was still on site. Since I had been caught stealing several times in the meantime, I now had to go to a correctional facility for two weeks. So when the day came, I went to the police station and from there they drove me there. Since I was constantly drinking alcohol, I was given a drug for a week to prevent any withdrawal symptoms. The drug always made me tired very quickly. So in the first week I slept almost all the time. In the second week I was relatively fit and could talk easily with the other three cellmates. It was quiet. Except for one or the other detainee who shouted something obscene from his cell.

After a week I was released and could hitchhike back to Amaus without any problems. A few months later, the court sentenced me to two years probation plus 2000 Euro in damages for the assault I had committed. I accepted the sentence with a detailed apology for what I did. From then on I had to see a probation officer every month. But I reached my mental limits here more and more often because of the alcohol addiction. It became very, very bleak for me mentally. My own situation just pulled me down completely. I just sat at the bus stop in the evening and rarely saw hope for myself. But I also realized that there were people who cared about how I was doing. I was often ashamed of my situation. That was often the reason for me not to hitchhike to Keith or Luke again. What helped me were small gestures. For example, when the kebab man brought me some pizza rolls with dip. That was something nice. Or getting money from a complete stranger for something to eat, or cigarettes, or beer. Nevertheless, I did not see the end yet.

My day began again and again with waking up as a homeless person. This thought wore me down. The people went past me. To work. To my home. To friends. To family. All of that was far, far away for me. I was trapped in my victim role and spiraled into very, very deep depression. It got to the point where I started to just avoid contact with people and let myself down. I said sentences like »Either you have beer for me, otherwise you don't have to chat me up at all.« So a completely antisocial phase, mixed with hatred and absolutely gloomy thoughts. I spoke to the birds in the trees. I just listened to Cypress Hill music over and over and over again every day. For years. In any weather. Outside in my sleeping bag. The music was often the last little light at the end of the tunnel for me.

I asked myself what I was doing on this planet. It was all shit anyway. I saw my mother, how she went away after shopping some meters away from me, without looking after me. Either she didn't want to see me in that state or she didn't have the strength. There were always two sides. I could no longer accept this state and just became extremely angry with myself. I flagellated myself for years. I sat on a seat of the bus stop. And was very, very desperate. Sitting there again one such day, I grabbed a piece of glass that was lying on the floor and cut my left palm several times with it. I didn't want to kill myself, but I wanted to feel pain. For years I suppressed it all and washed it down. My sadness should just stop. I fell into a state where I could no longer place what was happening. Then the police came, treated my wound and took me to the police station. I was just crying and said I wanted it all to stop. The police officers said »Don't worry, we'll help you«. Someone will be along shortly to give you a lift. I thought I was going to the nuthouse. But a small ambulance came and they drove me to a hospital in Bronau. There was a closed ward in the basement. It was a sort of catch basin for people with psychological or physical ailments. I was no longer alone with my sadness.

24. Not alone

I often thought my problems were big. There, at the latest, I realized that there were people struggling with much bigger issues. Most of these problems were often absorbed by the people who had the biggest hearts of all: the hospital staff. Respect! This is also where I learned to just look. To open my ears for the story of a stranger and to listen to what he or she had to tell. There were people here in incredibly difficult situations who finally dared to open up. I got several times the chance to let persons come into my heart and my head for a moment. And to dedicate myself to your topics as well. On the other hand, I also got the chance to open up to one or the other. To tell why I ended up here in the first place. And where I want to go. I wanted to go back to the specialized clinic for another, therapeutic attempt. There I saw what therapy could be like and was far from being what many told in horror stories. I remembered my first attempt at therapy and decided to pick up where I left off. It couldn't be that I was spinning my wheels so much and nothing would change. So I contacted the social workers and managed to get another attempt at therapy approved at the specialist clinic. Thus, after the detoxification, I was again driven by a civilian to the specialized clinic high up on the mountain. Again a medical first examination and the nasty procedure.

 The therapy started well. I arrived and had a good feeling.

However, after about three months I was secretly bullied by other clients. There were just clients who were mean. They imitated how I ate or how I moved. They did it in such a way that I couldn't report it. I was under immense psychological pressure. How was I going to make it through therapy like this if I was being secretly bullied? It got so bad for me that I developed psoriasis on my scalp. I used to have slight problems with dandruff. But now it developed extremely and it didn't go away on its own. Most clients were very into physical care and for me it would have been a shame if you discovered it. At least that's what I thought. So I had extreme pressure inside and just wanted to get rid of the psoriasis somehow. So in the evening, when it was actually time for a good night's sleep, I went into the bathroom with the hair clippers and started shaving off my hair in the center front. I just wanted to know how bad it was and at best scrape or wash it off. However, when I saw, that a hard crust had already formed, I panicked. Panic about the therapy, panic about my fate. No matter which way I took, there was no turning back. Maybe I could be understood, maybe not. At that moment I had to decide on a strategy for myself.

I decided to secretly pack a bag. Only for a »small« stay in the hospital. Outside it was deepest winter. Snowflakes were falling fast from the sky and outside it was freezing cold. But I didn't have a chance. I had to go through with it. So I got dressed, slipped out through the living room of the unit, leaning the sliding door so I could get back in if necessary. Then I hiked into the valley for over an hour through a moderate snowstorm. I arrived at the hospital around one o'clock in the morning. I stood there in the hallway of the emergency room with little light. A bit awkward with my bag and hood over my head. They asked me what was wrong and I said »I have really bad psoriasis and I really need treatment. I'm being treated at the clinic on the mountain. Please!«. Then simply came the request »Let me see«. I showed the doctor there my psoriasis and the answer was simply »This is not an emergency. We can't just treat you like that anyway without the clinic's approval. It is best that you just go back.« That's when I was really bummed out. Go back? With the Snowstorm out there? Tia, I had to go through that. »New strategy« thought up. Shit like that. I just decided to go back and confess everything. And hoped that they would understand me. Somehow everything went totally shit again.

So off I went, now up the mountain. Through the snowstorm. Up the mountain with the bag on my shoulder. I had arrived at 3:30 in the morning. Went in and checked in with the night guard and told him everything. I was then tested for drug and alcohol use. Since the tests were both negative, I was allowed to go to sleep for the time being. At seven thirty in the morning, the called crisis session began in the large therapy room. About thirty clients were now sitting in a circle. I sat in between with my jacket on and the hood pulled over my head. It was ultra awkward. The huge head therapist came in, sat down and sucked his menthol candy thoughtfully at first. At the same time, he first took a brief look at every single client at least once.

No one spoke and no one made a sound. Then I was instructed to tell my story. I told everything. Then I had to pull down my hood and show my head. It made me feel very insecure, but it was also liberating. After all, I was describing all my problems. Now came the other part. Of course, according to the rules of the specialized clinic, it was not allowed to just secretly go to the village at night. to make and secretly come back. Because: Of course, it could also be that one consumed drugs oneself or brought drugs with him. This was not acceptable for the clinic and for the protection of all. So it came down to the fact that I would have to go to detox at least once and then I could come back. This was also decided afterwards. I was promised to be admitted again after a clean treatment and provisional detoxification. Of course, I was extremely relieved about this. Psychologically, such information is important. After all, I now felt accepted, despite all the problems I was causing. In the context of the treatment, however, I could be sure that everything would be all right.

So I had to pack all my things and got the saved money paid out. A civilian of the facility drove me to one of the largest German centers for forensic psychiatry (LWL Center for Forensic Psychiatry Lippstadt). There I was referred to a detoxification by the doctor of the therapy. On the way to the clinic, we stopped by a dermatologist. There I was given an oily hair treatment for my scalp. That's how I found myself: in a locked ward of a forensic psychiatric hospital. The doors were really locked, by the way. Everything was monitored. The atmosphere reminded me of the movie »12 Monkeys«. A lot of white tiles. Cool and dulled.

25. Forensic psychiatry

Being a client in the closed ward was strange. I felt protected, from the »crazy world outside«. But actually, inside was the crazy world. I smeared the oily tincture on my scaly scalp several times a day. After a few days it healed. The other customers were very different. The strangest scenes took place. In the smoking room, of course, sat the smokers, with only one window tilted open because it was cold outside. Then one of the patients comes in, wrapped in probably three jackets, soccer scarf wrapped around his neck, wool cap on and says »Boar, it's warm here!!!« Then he went and made all the windows on tilt, so it really started to pull. Then there was a small TV corner with two small chairs next to each other. I sat there and watched TV. Then a female client sat down next to me and spontaneously started stroking my right leg. »Wow!!! Hands off« I said, stood up and reported the behavior to the front of dispatch. The central office was a glass house, where the staff could do their work protected. But you could also let them know because someone was going crazy. And that happened more often here. So I heard screams when I was in the room. A patient was probably going crazy, screaming around and was then probably »fixed«. She was probably restrained and given medication. Then I was sitting in the smoking room when an unbelievably nasty stench of rotting meat permeated the ward. It smelled really extremely disgusting. After a bit of research, we learned that it was an admitted homeless man.

He was found outside the clinic in a park. The man had an open wound on his leg, in which maggots were already crawling. It smelled really beastly. The man had to be treated in a hospital. Time passed and I thought about the fact that I could soon return to the specialized clinic. That's what I was concentrating on. After a week there was a new fellow patient on the ward whom I immediately found very interesting. She had an unusually interesting hairstyle. Her hair was styled up in the back. Unusually sexy. But what I also noticed was that she did not speak. After my observation absolutely with nobody. I also did not know what you had. Wanted to find out it, however, absolutely. »So«, I asked myself, »How should I proceed?« So over several days I tried to get into conversation with Her. And it's damn strange when you spoke something to someone and saw that they understood you.

But then didn't respond. Spooky. I packed into the psychological bag of tricks. I explained to her that it would be your decision alone to allow contact. She alone could decide to take my hand or not to take it. At that, I symbolically placed my hand on the table. That's when it happened: she took my hand. In my head I was breakdancing at that moment. I didn't really expect it and yet it happened. She looked just incredibly good to me and I was megahappy. So slowly we started talking and something like a little romance developed. On a closed ward of a forensic psychiatric hospital. Completely crazy.

Due to your situation at the time, you were only talkative to a limited extent. But that was not bad. After your parents visited a few times, her father gave me to understand that the relationship was already doomed to failure. I took that on board, but at the time I couldn't do much with this information. Now I had a girlfriend and we were both patients in this ward at the same time. This became quite strange, because the place was so inappropriate for getting to know each other. One day, as we were sitting together having our lunch, the patient who needed to be petted actually came up to us. Then she suddenly stabbed my schnitzel with her fork without warning, as if she wanted to kill it and then take it away. I never fought for a schnitzel so quickly. I held the schnitzel with fork and knife at the same time on the plate and admonished »Hey! There remains nicely there! Go away!« Then she let go of the Schnitzel and went away again to your place and ate calmly continued. Then I stood up briefly and complained to the »waiter« at the aquarium about »the behavior of the guest«. Lunch could now be eaten.

After two weeks on this ward, I was transferred to another ward. On this one, the patients didn't have quite as severe symptoms. Now I finally found a girlfriend and had to leave. What was I supposed to do? Because I had neither an apartment nor a job. So I also had no address or telephone number that I could have given her. So I moved to the other station. But I was worried because I wanted to go to therapy again. After another week on the other ward, one of the nurses handed me a piece of paper from her. It had her address and phone number on it. Yay! But then I got some bad news from one of the social workers. Namely, that the clinic had decided not to admit me again. Further: They would have to dismiss me now directly, because I would not show any symptoms that would justify a further treatment. I guess they couldn't make any more money with me. And there they were again, my problems. So they just abandoned me with the second therapy attempt and then they even threw me out the door. I was really, really flabbergasted. How was I supposed to get on the right track? How could I manage without help? I was allowed to pack my bag again as a hobby. And I called my girlfriend and told her the current status. Then I had to get out. As a reminder, I was still on probation for the assault. This meant that I still had to report regularly to the probation officer. So I had to go back to Amaus very quickly but forced. Also because this probation officer was the only one who knew what was going on.

26. Again without destination

As soon as I was released, I stocked up on beer and took the train back to Amaus. When I arrived there, I already had a good one. So I walked into town and looked for the probation officer, but didn't find him. Okay, I thought. Now you could think what you wanted about that. So I just went back to the supermarket of my wet dreams and stood there with my bag. Planlessly in the nowhere. To my delight, an ex-speaker of Alcoholics Anonymous came up to me, whom I also knew from one of the hospital stays. I guess he was no longer with the »AAs« and invited me for a whiskey-cola. So I took my bag and just went along. Maybe I could have stayed overnight at his apartment as an emergency solution. We went to the city center upstairs to a pub.

There he really ordered one whiskey-cola after the other for us. After a few rounds he became strange, babbling something about having rich parents and therefore believing he was being watched by the secret service. Then, from one second to the next, he suddenly said, »Go!« So I should see about gaining land. Apparently he had a film break and could not cope with his situation himself. Since I didn't feel like fighting or anything, I took my bag, thanked him and left. When I was outside and made it down the stairs, I got gasping for breath. Now came what had to come. In the fresh air, the whiskey and coke really, really knocked me out. I took my bag and walked through the city still without a destination. I thought, I will find already something to sleep. Sometimes I walked just to get tired. That way, falling asleep – no matter where – is not so hard anymore. Then I lost myself in thoughts and daydreamed. I felt strange, a little dark before my eyes. I became absent for a moment.

Then I came back to my senses. I was suddenly at the supermarket but without my bag! Where was my goddamn bag? With all my clothes and worst of all: the address of my first girlfriend? This couldn't be true! I looked around but the bag was no longer there. I must have run somewhere in the film tear for about two hours and forgot to take my bag again. And that's what I had now! What should I do? Now I was not only without a place to stay, but once again I lost everything I had. Once again I needed help. So I went to the police station. They let me in and I told everything. I said in my distress that I would bang my head live here on the counter if they wouldn't let me. Sure, not necessarily great but I needed my stuff back. No matter how, »I really need to go to the hospital. Only there can one me help now. Please, I lost my bag and I really need it back. It's totally important.« This was extreme, of course, but I knew I needed help now, not tomorrow or later. Now.

And at this point I also saw in the police the real helper »Don't worry Mr. Fog Frost, we have never let you down and we are not doing so now. Please come to your senses.

Someone will come to pick you up in a moment.« In fact, someone came by with a small ambulance that took me to the Bronau hospital, strapped into the back of the seat. On the way there, I was relieved about the help but on the other hand really nervous because I didn't have my bag back yet. I was admitted to the hospital. I was so upset about my situation that I could not sleep properly. The next day, a civilian actually came and brought me my bag, which I thought I had lost forever! I could not believe it. He really brought me my bag! And nothing was missing. Finally I could call my girlfriend and tell her where I was and how I was doing. On the phone she said that her father was still not happy about our relationship.

I gave everything on the phone. So I wanted to finally have a girlfriend who understands me completely. I could win she despite all circumstances further for me. This gave me a incredible mental strength. To know that I was able to win a girlfriend over. That a direction is emerging for me from this. After a few days in the hospital and the re-established contact with the probation officer, I got the opportunity to a shelter for homeless people, in the not too far away town of Kohsfeld to accommodate. Thus I had a roof over the head and with the unemployment assistance a kind regular »Pocket money«. That was divided up so that you didn't spend it all at once. I moved into a room for two people and met Bernd. Bernd was a trained interior designer and used to have his own company for kitchen construction.

He had clients like Rudi Assauer (a legendary german football pro) and proudly showed me all his letters and qualification papers. He was very articulate and taught me a bit of rhetoric. He had a lot of black money and sometimes gave me money for nothing in return. He also gave me diazepam and we drank freshly squeezed orange juice with liquor in our room. And talked about different topics. He was quite cunning and showed me how to have a good time. While others were biting into a dry slab of bread at breakfast, he was happily and relaxedly grabbing salmon on a bun. He also showed me what you can save on in everyday life. So he said sentences like »Buy the cheapest shaving cream and the cheapest razor!« One of his good tips. A very nice, helpful but also cunning person.

When I lived there for a few weeks, I simply invited my girlfriend so that we could just meet. The accommodation was of course not a romantic environment for a date. That's why I preferred to visit you at home in your hometown of Flippstadt, where I have been twice so far. At least from this address. It became a long distance relationship at first. After a few weeks in this facility, the pressure of addiction overtook me. I started drinking way too much every day, even though consumption was strictly forbidden in the facility. At some point, I blew my cover and they kicked me out the door. I went to the local train station and met someone there who had a daily job but also liked to drink a lot. He said I could stay with him for a while and sleep on the couch. I accepted the offer and stayed with him for about two weeks. My job on weekends – because that was the only time he was home – was to run out and buy a bottle of Doppeloxer (herbs liquor). He even gave me some money for that. On the second weekend my girlfriend also visited me there. She probably realized that my situation could not really change that way.

The eternal same environment of other alcoholics could not bring me further. She said she would drive up and I should just get on the next train and follow her and call her when I had arrived. She would then pick me up at the station in Flippstadt. So she went first with the train back home and I followed her with a train later. At a stopover in Portmund bought me for 50€ heroin. But I did not manage to seal myself with it. I was afraid that I would smoke too much of it in the drunkenness and would die from it. So I packed the stuff and took the train to Flippstadt. When I arrived I called her. She came after fifteen minutes and picked me up in a small Renault Twingo. Before we left, I honestly showed her the shorn and she insisted that I throw that shit away. And I did. Emotionally I stood here between, everything will be fine and everything was already very, very shit.

27. Second pad

So we drove to her family. Once there, it must have been a weird scene for the parents. I came directly with bag and baggage around the corner. So according to the motto "Okay, now I live with you." There the father asked me simply times for a discussion under four eyes. During this conversation I told him that I was a child of divorce and had had problems with the law here and there, but now I was just trying to start from scratch. There he said to me very dryly »You have no problems. Others have some.« This statement was a good comparison to motivate me. And at least a little bit to bring me back to reality. Since most of the family wanted to go on vacation to the Netherlands in a week, they decided to just take me with them. I was very impressed by the family atmosphere. It seemed to me as if one dealt in principle rather openly with problems. But already in such a way that nothing was brought out into the open.

 So I was able to stay there and after a week the father went with all of us for a week's vacation in the Netherlands to a campsite. My girlfriend and I just slept in an igloo tent in front of the parents' caravan. In the caravan slept the father, the mother and the little sister. The brother of my girlfriend, stayed at home and watched over the house. The vacation was really beautiful. We took a bike ride into the village and walked along the beach. Really romantic. In the evening in the tent, when it was already dark, I turned me a joint and smoked this cozy on. My girlfriend didn't mind that I smoked pot. It made her apparently nothing. When the vacation was over and we arrived back in Flippstadt at the family home, the »father-in-law« helped me find an apartment. My parents also gave me some older furnishings so I didn't have to buy everything new. I got the apartment paid by the city office and had to become active as return of course. So there was from me still the desire to catch up the secondary school diploma.

I could definitely try to do that there. From then on I attended an institution like the BOZ in Amaus and tried again to get my secondary school leaving certificate. The apartment had almost 55 square meters and was located on the second floor of a row house settlement. From time to time my girlfriend also slept there. She was very caring and smart. So she completed the »voluntary social year« in a kindergarten, which she needed for her intended professional career. She introduced me to some of her friends. Sometimes I got the opportunity to buy directly larger quantities of good hash. Instead of too expensive with too small quantities. So it didn't take long until I started selling here and there, so that the consumption basically financed itself. One day, my girlfriend invited me to go to a disco in Munster. There where always very well and gladly celebrated. I didn't know about this, I had only heard about it. Still on the way there I emptied a bottle of apple schnapps. And that without getting excessively drunk. In the club we celebrated more or less intensively. In the morning we were stranded at the train station, but it was still quite a long time before trains would run again. So she just ran to an ATM, picked up some money and called a cab for both of us. The cab drove us »home«. The relationship was harmonious at first. My greed for hash became great. So it wasn't long before I was smoking a bong in the morning before class. It did not remain only with the consumption of hash or Weed. The consumption of beer soon took on a very extreme level. I just became reckless and naive again. Through a small, steady clientele, I was able to counter-finance my consumption for a while. The relationship lasted just under a year and a half, but my behavior was unbearable to the relationship. The tensions became great. I developed psychological problems again.

My greed for consumption and the accompanying loss of control were an extreme disappointment for my girlfriend. She thought I could develop positively. I thought so, too, at first. And yet I allowed the addiction to hold me hostage took. I allowed myself to lose my first, real friend because I couldn't manage to turn things around. I never forgot the day when she started crying in despair, went out, got on her bike and rode off. I knew then, this is the end of the relationship. And it hurt like hell. I felt empty inside. As if the addiction had sucked me dry like a vampire. On the same day, her father went with her to pick up everything that was still important to her. There was no big farewell talk. They just picked up everything and drove away. I didn't deserve much more at that moment. My apartment just a remnant of a relationship – as my father had foreseen – doomed to failure. My now ex-girlfriend was by no means without empathy. She even drove me again a few weeks later to the forensic clinic where I was going to complete my self-requested detox. I did not know of any other people who could have driven me there. She even visited me again in detox and played pool with me. I suspected that she was saying goodbye to me internally in this last get-together, not showing it, but I felt it. Through the sale, of course, I met a plethora of addicted people. After the two weeks of detox, it wasn't long before I started selling the rest of the apartment items. In between, I heard from a Colleagues that my parents would look for me because they were worried. At first I thought it was a rumor until they were actually in the car ahead of me near the train station because they were looking for me.

That seemed strange to me. They probably told me that I had been run over by a truck. I could understand that this did not leave the parents calm. I also had no contact with them for a long time. So we drove to the apartment or what was left of it. In the meantime I was sure that the electricity had already been switched off. My stepfather at the time then discovered that only the toaster was broken and that the fuse kept blowing out. After a short discussion, they later drove home. I remained alone in this apartment. The colleagues and I wanted to have a little party in the apartment, knowing that I would have to leave soon. And where I could go, I did not know yet. Without further ado, we organized a small party, with medium to heavy consumption of various substances. Almost around midnight, another colleague came by with a woman I didn't know. The two simply wanted to have a room for themselves. So I offered the bedroom, there the two could have your peace. We listened to some loud music in the living room. Unfortunately, the development of the meeting between the two guests went in a completely unexpected direction. The woman suddenly wanted to leave. Apparently you didn't completely agree with your colleague's demands. The colleague was not apparent to me at first apparently on drugs. What exactly happened in the room, I did not know, only I suddenly got how the woman ran stark naked from the apartment.

Then I was extremely perplexed because that also meant that the guy wanted something that she definitely didn't want. When this action took place, of course, the entire party crowd said goodbye and looked for the far. The colleague who brought the woman with him suddenly threw her clothes out of my window onto the lawn. There it was in the morning about three o'clock. The naked woman, now in a state resembling a panic attack, knocked on the doors across the street at the AWO (an

Organisation, assisted living) and shouted »Help, police!!! Help!!!« So it didn't take long for neighbors and the AWO to take notice of the woman. I, on the other hand, was struggling to flush away any remaining substances in the toilet. So this whole »party« got completely out of hand. The police came and I was packed into a patrol car in handcuffs right in front of the neighborhood. My apartment was searched for possible evidence. The woman later told the police station that the colleague tried to rape her. After I communicated that the two came to me hand in hand and both obviously went into the bedroom amicably, I could leave.

When I re-entered the apartment, I just felt out of place. The environment became like a place of failure for me overall. It took a few days before I was invited to an interview with the landlord. There one announced to me then not completely unexpectedly the notice. A few days later I simply packed a bag with stuff again and went with it to a colleague, to whom I had already sold something a few times. With him I could put my clothes provisionally. This colleague lived in assisted living and I was able to sleep there a few times. I soon found new shelter through a contact at the probation service. Again in a facility for homeless men.

28. Little blue pill

In the dormitory there were several floors and rooms of different sizes. Some rooms were for one person, others for two. I got a place in a room for two people, which I shared with another young gentleman. The roommate appeared to be smart, reading Nietzsche. He generally always looked for side jobs in gambling halls. In order to be able to plunder the coffers without much effort. When his older brother visited him, they played chess together. Of course, the consumption of alcohol or drugs was forbidden in this institution. And yet almost everyone did it secretly, as I did. In order to get back into the working world, I looked for a job. A company that sold and refilled printer cartridges wanted to give me a chance. So I started there and got directly from the boss the keys for the business premises and the code for the alarm system. The work was fine for me, but the alcohol addiction came closer again. We once went on a week's vacation to the Czech Republic with the facility. That was really great. Until there was a real ruckus in one of the rooms in the evening. That's when the social workers got suspicious. In a clarification meeting with all the people, it came out that one of the roommates had regularly beaten his roommate so that he would do whatever he wanted.

This, of course, violated the rules of the facility, so the return trip was quite quiet. The violent guy was immediately released. Out of the facility, it actually lived quite well. One day there was a blond girl who looked incredibly good and visited the other boys. I was a little jealous, but didn't have high hopes. Also because I was still busy with my addiction. In the evening, one of the colleagues who visited her came to me and gave me a piece of paper with her phone number. That was of course very cool. I was currently having a little romance with another girl. But this girl got weird. She asked me things like »What would you do if I threw myself in front of a train?« So I told her »You can go now. I have no desire for such mind games.« So she left. The social worker who was present sat in his office with the door open and watched what was happening.

Immediately after I threw she out, I went to the office, pulled my phone joker out and called the blonde beauty. We had a date directly on the same evening and it sparked directly. I learned that she came from the East, liked to dance and now lived with her father in. The father could not stand me because I did not leave a good impression with my alcoholism. Nevertheless, I always wanted to deal with it honestly, as far as I could. That's why I felt like he was always against me. My addiction level was again bigger. So one day I met a colleague who was also bare. And I was also short of pocket. I'd had the job at the printer store for just two weeks, so I made the decision to walk into the store late at night. I took a laptop, a bit of change and blew it with the colleague. The next day, the (now) ex-boss contacted the facility and demanded the laptop in return for waiving criminal charges. So I went there with a social worker as an intermediary, handed over the laptop, apologized. Of course, the employment relationship was terminated. Another incredibly stupid action. I had a falling out with my new girlfriend, and she probably realized how addicted I was already on the road here.

In the context of the conflict, I needed distraction and I just wanted to visit another girl who lived a few kilometers away. I hitchhiked there without much ulterior motive. Arrived there, after several kilometers, she gave me to understand that between us nothing would run. Again a stupid action. Disappointed with my situation, I went away and bought canned beer. Oh you savior in need. I just hitchhiked off and ended up in some town. There a guy in a small, red 15 mph car with a foxtail on the antenna stopped and said simply »Get in, we'll have a drink!« I got in and we drove to an apartment in a terraced housing estate. There were two Russian compatriots there, probably drinking buddies. And they simply invited me to drink. After a few shots, however, it became too much for me and I preferred to go back to the facility in Flippstadt.When I was standing on the street and wanted to hitchhike, the alcohol really kicked in and I lost consciousness. The lights just went out.

I woke up in a cell at the police station and was pretty messed up. All I wanted to do was hitchhike to Flippstadt.

When I asked how I had gotten here, I was told »We received a call and were told that a person almost ran into a truck while trying to hitchhike. But you were very lucky. This was clearly life-threatening. Not just for you. A social worker will be coming to pick you up in a minute.« There really was a social worker from the facility coming to pick me up. Namely, the chief. When he arrived, they told him the story and he drove back to the facility with me. Once at the facility, he immediately made it clear that this would have serious consequences for me. One conversation further, he said that my behavior would pose a risk to the facility and that I would therefore have to leave the facility on the same day. Again, I had managed to steer my fate in an undetermined direction. Dumb and dumber. So I packed my clothes again and came back to my »clientele«. Only this time I was the one who asked for help. But things turned out a little different here than I thought. The local probation officer gave me a tip where I could stay. Not in a sterile residential area, but at least a room in the attic. In a house that was known to be inhabited by the worst alcoholics in town.

From the office I got the promise that the rent is taken over at first. So I could keep my head above water with Hartz IV (money from the state). The contact with the blonde friend from the East did not end at all, so we became closer again. This then became a relationship. She actually somehow managed to arrange a sofa bed for my birthday out of the blue. Until now, I had simply slept in a sleeping bag and on a sleeping mat. It was colder outside again and the heating in the house was constantly broken. So I often had to help myself with a fan heater. The blonde friend always stood by me, no matter what happened to me. We were in love and she looked after me. And besides that, there was the addiction that often kept me under control. I remembered how I slept secretly with her one night, in her room at her parents' house. Although I was not allowed to be there. Then I had to go to the toilet in the basement very urgently, sneaked down to the toilet. Suddenly the door opened and the mother caught sight of me for a moment and was startled. She went briskly upstairs. And I secretly but very quickly behind. I got dressed very quickly. As soon as I was dressed, I heard loud, indignant complaining from my father, who was already making his way to your room.

 I quickly opened the window and jumped out. I ran and the father scolded me. That would have been impertinent and so on. Yes, exactly. Blah blah blah. Nothing was normal in the alcoholic house where I lived. There was a little courtyard outside. So to get to your room, you had to go through this courtyard. Downstairs lived someone, sort of the »Caretaker« with his dog: a large St. Bernard. The dog called »Max« barked loudly, but was very kind-hearted. Once, while it was still warm outside, I came into the courtyard where there was already a bottle of Korn on the table in the morning and a crate of beer on the floor next to it. Next to it a self-built apparatus for »smoking buckets«. »Bucket smoking« is a way to smoke pot. Just a damn bad place. Probably the worst I had ever seen. But I was addicted to everything. Especially just alcohol. When another boy moved in right next to me, I was soon hooked on speed, too. So addicted, in fact, that lousy scenes began to play out. My girlfriend was visiting and sitting in my room. But I was sitting in the other room and I was taking a hit of speed. Just to be on it like hell. Next door waited They on me, but I did not come over. Instead, it was more important for me to sit with this guy and pull one line after another with him.

Then we suddenly heard a clattering next door. Then I walked past and saw that my girlfriend, in desperation, had punched a hole in the window with a curtain rod. She was just tired of watching me ignore all that. That I let my addiction control me like a lemming. She really did everything she could to somehow get me away from it. This situation opened my eyes at least a little bit.

A few days later. I met »Bo« who also sold dope. After I became friends with him, we went through a wild time. So »Bo« came to one of the colleagues in Flippstadt-South with the motorcycle but: without helmet. So on quite cool. He took me with him and we rode the motorcycle bluntly to his apartment, which was a little outside. A kind of shared apartment for students. We listened to house music there and kept blaring away. A few hours later we drove the motorcycle but again without helmet to the local supermarket. Are purely and bought bluntly canned beer. The beer we drank in front of the store and then just left on the motorcycle again. He showed me how to sell »stuff« inconspicuously. When I was at home in the evening and just wanted to sleep, someone came along whom I had always considered trustworthy. He wanted to buy a small piece hash on combo for a cell phone as a deposit.

Can be done. So far no thing. I gave him a small piece, he said he'd bring me the money later or tomorrow. Then he went. Then I lay down. I was almost asleep when there was a knock at the door. »Hey, I want to give you the money back.« I already thought that it must have been late, because I was already extremely tired. Okay, I thought, and opened the door for him. But as soon as I opened the door, it slammed inward and three strange boys stood in the room. One threw me on my sofa bed and the other promptly held a knife to my neck. »Where's your stuff?« I pointed »very nicely« to my jacket and got rid of dope for 400€. The persons spoke only broken German, no English and also no Dutch. And the supposedly trustworthy colleague took his cell phone and left with the others. Apparently he had debts with his own colleagues and had to make a pawn sacrifice. I could have talked myself into it. Well, it wasn't pleasant. So much for that. I met a lot of people in Flippstadt. Addiction expanded my own stupidity mercilessly.

Could also remember an afternoon I spent with another very cool colleague. The kind of colleague who, while walking through downtown, started taking a jacket off a sales rack and just kept on running with me. One of the saleswomen called the police and we took to our heels. In a small alley he just gave me his backpack and said »Here, take care of it until I'm out again«. Then he took off. I then looked at the contents of the backpack and found fishing dungarees inside. It wasn't chilly, but of course I had reached my fun level again and put the things on. In addition, a megacool sunglasses. Also in the backpack: two bottles of Jägermeister. With it I made myself then also the way to the colleague Rigoles. One street further I saw how the good one was collected by the police. At Rigoles always met the older generation men with mostly failed existences. When I had made my entrance in my special outfit, I unpacked the two large bottles of Jägermeister.

That's when the pack gradually began to disperse. One probably already suspected that this would not have a good end. Regardless of the direction, Rigoles was known for his legendary record collection. He liked to play real classics like the Duck Dance. So after about thirty minutes, there were only two of us left and we started drinking Jägermeister. I woke up, it was dark and I really had to go to the bathroom. I tried to get up and slammed into the marble tabletop of Rigoles. The tabletop broke and banged loudly on the floor. Must probably so against six o'clock in the morning. Rigoles came in from his bedroom quite annoyed »Oh no, now you've broken the good table. You'll definitely have to pay for it. Seventy euros at least.« I said it was no problem, I would pay for the damage. When I came back from the toilet, Rigoles said »You, I need a little rest now and must ask you to go.« I got from him another can of beer and exactly one euro and he let me pull away. Was I there a poor sow. But I also gave myself everything I could get.

Another time at the train station, I asked a man who looked to me like someone who consumed something if he could give me anything to seal. The man reached into his pocket and gave me a blue, small pill. Not knowing what it was, I took it and just downed beer. After about an hour, one of the colleagues from the assisted living house came over. I talked to him and told him something else. Then I got tunnel vision, but kept talking. Suddenly my eyes went black. I woke up and was lying on a bed in the hospital. Again, I was wearing only a surgical gown and my head was very, very heavy. There was my girlfriend with me and she looked sadly and worriedly into my eyes »Please never, never do something like that again, do you hear me?« I was on it so much that I just wanted to beam away over and over again. I had no idea of what happened. When I was released a day later, I went with her to the colleague I was still talking to at the station. He was very disappointed in me. He was also worried about my life. That I was ready to just give up on myself.

I had already smoked heroin on tin in between and knew how it feels when the drug just puts a warm blanket around your body. You no longer have or feel any pain. You are extremely sedated by the drug. This is what makes it so dangerous. Back to the story. I went to his place and sat on his couch. At first we had a halfway good conversation. I was still conscious. Then I got a circulatory collapse, so much so that I just let water. Total blackout. I was no longer conscious and there were no more signs of life, even according to him. So, in his fear, he called 911 (he called 112 in germany) directly. Of course, I was incredibly embarrassed and ashamed. And shameful could also be the title of the next chapter.

29. German Bundeswehr

In this seemingly perspective-less time, the day of days came. I received mail from the Bundeswehr. The air base in Goslar called for me. The hole in the window of my room was mended, the girlfriend calmed down, and I was allowed to go there by train. Great. Once there, we all got new, refurbished clothes. I was the oldest in the room, so I had »command« for our room. The boots did not fit, the steel toe cap scraped the ankles of the toes. Everyone was given a locker. We were taught how to make the bed and how to hang and put the clothes in the locker sensibly. We were also shown in detail how to clean the room. The first month flew by. In the second month, it became more challenging. I had to fight with addictive pressure again. After two weeks I decided to simply stay in Flippstadt after the weekend and not return to the Bundeswehr. I had to take the train every time and I wanted to spend more time with my girlfriend. It was a Wednesday or Thursday, my girlfriend and I were on the way to the 1 room apartment. In the hallway, almost upstairs, were two men I didn't know. The men asked me if I was who I was and told me my name.

 Then the men identified themselves as military police and ordered me to open the room so that I could take my things with me to duty. First, I was searched like a felon against the wall. Then I had to pack my bag. I was not allowed to take canned beer with me. Afterwards I was allowed to say goodbye to my girlfriend. They drove me, first to a Bundeswehr barracks, which I didn't know, and locked me in a room with a bed, table and chair. I had to sit on the chair and was not allowed to lie down or sleep. As soon as my eyes fell shut, the door opened and a soldier shouted »Airman Nebelfrost, no sleeping here! Stay awake!«. It went on like that all night. In the morning I was really exhausted. Then I had to re-cover the bed, although I was not allowed to sleep in it. Pure chicanery. Then they drove me back to the barracks, where from now on I was only allowed to carry out my duties under observation. In other words: I was allowed to clean »my weapon« but not to use it. Thus began the dilemma. A few days later: in the evening the comrades went out to get cigarettes and a bottle or two of beer. I came from the supermarket with two carrier bags full of spirits. In the smoking room I started to finish the evening with a beer and a bottle of »Blue Angel«. Literally. In the days before, my locker had already been filled with an uncontrolled large quantity of empty beer cans. So I became again scourge of alcohol addiction and fate took its course. I woke up in the morning, but I was not lying on my mattress on my side. It smelled full of urine. The parlor mates told me that I was »finished« and »You peed in your own bed.« I was just shocked.

Shocked by what addiction was doing to me. How could I

sink so low? I went to my locker, but it was locked. The key was gone. I wanted to change and had to get a pair of bolt cutters from somewhere. So I went down to the guard's office lightly dressed and told them what had happened. They probably already knew and gave me a bolt cutter. I picked my lock, changed clothes and brought the bolt cutters back down. It was clear to me that morning that this was not going to bear fruit. For one thing, I had a criminal record for assault. For another, my daily alcohol requirement was far too high. All this shame in front of myself. The addiction was too strong. I didn't stand a chance on my own. I had to admit it to myself. So I called in sick at morning roll call, but still had to take part in a theory block. In this theory block, the other »comrades« started to talk shit about me. The old fear broke over me like a thunderstorm with thunder and lightning. »Bedwetter« I heard someone whisper. I sank into the ground and could no longer stand myself. My face was petrified and I pretended not to hear all the whispering. And yet those involved knew I heard it.

When I was finally allowed to interview the highest-ranking sergeant major after the theory unit, I put all my cards on the table. The answer was »T5 – retired. You go now, pack all your things and bring them back to where you got them. That's it for you. All the best for your health.« So I booted off, returned my things and took the train back to Flippstadt to my girlfriend at the time.

30. Medical opinion

Back to the loft. Since the money for the rent was still being transferred to me at this point, I of course didn't have to transfer it, but could use it. So it happened that the lease was terminated by the landlord. On the level of addiction I did not care. Due to several minor offenses in which I was caught, I was threatened with a new court hearing. Since at that time I performed almost all my actions under the influence of alcohol sometimes more or sometimes less successfully, the court ordered a medical report. So there was this one day when a doctor came to visit me in my teeny-tiny attic flat to examine me completely. It must have been strange for him. I could only offer him a small chair to sit on, I didn't even have a table yet. He insisted at first that I just sit down or lie down and tell him my life story. I found that quite interesting. Then he examined me physically and felt me up. Then I had to go through a few motor tests. The whole thing lasted about four hours. For me quite a long time. The clinical picture was multiple dependency and dissocial personality disorder.

31. From the street to the girlfriend

My girlfriend was now able to move into her own apartment, but she didn't actually want me to live with her, she wanted me to do something myself. So she was already interested in me learning to develop my own plans and implement them. This approach was completely understandable. I was completely naive and used to the homeless life by now. Once you have immersed yourself in this world and experienced this form of deceptive freedom, it is all the more difficult to escape it. It's like a bad mood: the longer you dwell on it, the worse and longer this phase becomes. So I often went to the station again, listened to Cypress Hill again and drank one canned beer after another. Often I drank about ten cans until noon. In between again and again also hard stuff.

It was just miserable. I was ashamed in front of my girlfriend, but couldn't make the jump. I wanted to be alone in the phases of drinking and sobering up. Not to be a burden to anyone. The flashbacks to failed attempts at therapy made me sad and depressed. Every day, all I saw was my own past. My siblings who I didn't see in real life. I could only imagine their current appearance. One evening – drunk again – I went from the station down the street to the left and saw on the right side of the street a small mountain with furniture for the bulky waste. There was also a dark red couch. I just grabbed it and pulled it across the street into the bushes. And then I just lay down on it and slept. It was there at just the right moment. In the morning, when I woke up, I stayed there for a while. Then a man from the railroad came and handed me a big parasol over the fence. »As rain protection. Please!« – »Thank you!«, I said and stuck the umbrella into the ground in such a way that the couch was now protected even from the rain. I slept on the couch for about fourteen days, when the sleeping place was disposed of by the city. Every now and then I managed to stay overnight at my girlfriend's house. She became quite sociable in the meantime.

On the one hand, she thought I was old enough and needed to know where I could go or who I belonged to. But on the other hand, she was incredibly caring and worried enormously about other people. Not just about me, but in general. One evening, when I once again didn't make it »home«, I laid down on a »new mattress« again in the bushes. This time just drunk in the rain. I was very exhausted and wanted only one thing: sleep. She looked for me then probably late in the evening and then discovered me lying on this mattress in the bushes. I heard only sentences like »Man Jan, so You can't do that! I'm worried about you!« and »You're going to die with pneumonia!« For me it sounded just dimly like in a dream. I was stoned and didn't really notice anything about it. A little rain, a little fresh air, I didn't mind.

Some days later. Then I was away for about a week. So she

didn't even know if I was coming back at all. I was out drinking and took onions from some garden and ate them raw. I was just hungry for something spicy. Then I wanted to go to the warm place. I went to the row house where my girlfriend lived, but she wasn't there. However, I somehow got into the hallway and then just laid down at the top of the hallway and slept. She came home later. The whole hallway must have smelled immensely of onions. She somehow got me into the apartment and I could sleep with her despite the stench. In the morning I still stank »like hell«. There was of course a conversation between her and me in the morning according to the circumstances but: She was never unfair to me. On the contrary: I was unfair to her. After some time she offered me to live with her.

This was apparently not enough for my addiction. I lost myself again and again in the drunkenness and at the station. With a colleague in the residential district of a social In turn, I got to know another dealer. A week later I learned that he had been stabbed in his hallway. Just like in a movie. Traumatic and yet reality. The events of that environment, among the people I knew, just got ugly. And I wondered what life was all about. I just considered it for me in between to just stay in your apartment. Even if the next gas station was just down the street.

So every now and then I managed to stay in the apartment. Okay, but sometimes not. Then I went out with money for two »starter cans« and just tried again to get more money for more alcohol. For my birthday in 2013, she came up with something special: She secretly invited the whole family: Mom, the stepfather and mysiblings except for my younger brother. And one of the colleagues at the time, who still played the guitar. It was just great to see everyone again. It was probably just important to her that I finally got the feeling that they loved me again. And that worked. The apartment became much more than just a place to spend the night. Here I could retreat and think.

32. Court date

The day came when I was summoned to the court hearing as a defendant. I had prepared for the day of the trial for weeks. But not to trick or lie. I asked myself for three weeks in my girlfriend's apartment »What would my goals be?« One of my first goals was to just stay in the apartment every day. Not to drink. To reflect on why I was often going in circles. To question what I could accomplish in life. Without thinking about what I was doing before. What all could I accomplish if given the chance? I looked outside into the trees and wondered what I loved to play as a little boy. Why was I the way I was, and where could I go from here?

I was young and by no means too old not to try after all. During this phase, I decided to completely rebuild my strategy. I said to myself »No matter where this path would take me. No matter with which people. No matter if I had to leave someone behind, like my girlfriend. It was only important for me.« So I remembered the therapy attempts and realized that this would be the only true path. I had to start over. I would use it as an opportunity. It had to be.

My probation was on the line due to many minor offenses. I disregarded the obligation to report to the probation officer several times. The offenses were: several small thefts and credit card fraud. Now the time had come and I found myself over punctual for my court date. The judge began to read the charges. I was questioned and did not deny any of my actions. The judge looked over them again. Then he said »Almost all of your offenses took place under the influence of alcohol. The expert opinion showed, among other things, a multiple addiction. If you had the choice between a prison sentence or therapy, which would you choose?« I argued »If I were to serve a prison sentence, I would get out with money saved, I probably wouldn't have learned anything, and I would very likely start drinking again. So I'm asking you to really give me the very longest therapy you can give me. Thank you.«

The judge thought for a moment and then, fortunately for me, announced the sentence: »correctional system« according to paragraph 64. (Long time therapy instead of jail) I was very relieved and it was a huge load off my mind. The sentence meant placement in a rehab facility for addicted offenders. I thus received the ticket for a long but extremely professional therapy. Now I just had to get an appointment. After all, you couldn't get a place and go right away. Everything still had to be organized be. So I didn't know where I was going for detox or where the therapy was going to be. I was just very, very happy that I got this chance. This changed a lot of things for me.

From now on, I took it easy. I still consumed beer a few times at the station, but not as often, for as long and as much as before. Now I also got to know other people who had noticed me because of my manner. Among other things, I got to know Steve, who offered me cigarettes from time to time. At some point he outed himself as homosexual, but I didn't find that bad. Steve must have had rich parents and even took care of the disposal of the old things from the facility I was once thrown out of. A really nice guy. A few weeks later I got a letter telling me exactly when and where I had to go to detox.

And here it comes: Since I didn't have a driver's license yet, Steve drove me with a scooter from Flippstadt to the specialized clinic for detoxification. And that was in winter. So we both froze our asses off on the scooter. And my girlfriend on the bus with my bag behind. When I said goodbye to this wonderful person, my girlfriend took me to the clinic. After about an hour she left as well. And I was again in a closed ward. This time with the goal of really going through with it.

33. Therapy Preparation - Detoxification

The opportunity I got here had a huge meaning for me. I understood that I was given the chance to change my life for good. Until then, I could only guess at the circumstances and requirements. But it was clear to me that I would go this way. I no longer wanted to be steered by my long-time partner – the addiction. Instead, I wanted to go through life in a self-determined way. With only 65kg (and i was 1,90cm, so one could no longer speak of body weight), I was admitted to detoxification. The closed ward was in the middle of a move to another building. So the very next day I went to another building. The fellow patients were tolerable throughout. I began the gentle introduction to normal food intake. Later, I occasionally dared to eat fresh fruit. A new patient came to the ward. He was always afraid that he would be forbidden to consume coffee. So he constantly filled himself with cold coffee in empty deposit bottles and stashed them in the smoking room. A funny oddball with a mullet leaned hairstyle. So that the future specialized clinic could evaluate whether I fit into their concept, I wrote a curriculum vitae on the advice of a social worker.

 I adjusted myself inwardly to the fact that I would simply go my own way. Wherever that might be. Because I suspected that the therapy would not be easy, I decided here in detox to quit smoking for good. I felt it was a personal weakness. I wanted to complete the therapy either completely, that is, without all addictive substances, or not at all. It was absolutely no fun anymore, it just disgusted me. As inspiration I read the book »Finally Non-Smoker« by Allen Carr. I couldn't stand it any longer: pretending it was cool to smoke. After almost three months in detox, I finally learned the name and location. For me, a completely new place that I did not know yet. Even further away from parents, relatives and acquaintances. So I already knew from the previous trials that the initial separation from the familiar environment was part of the therapeutic concept. A civilian picked me up one day and drove me directly to the specialized clinic.

34. Inpatient therapy

The clinic itself was located on a mountain, several meters away from the city down in the valley. The clinic was staffed exclusively by very well-trained personnel. The number of clients was always around thirty. After I got there, I was assigned another patient to act as a godfather. The »godfather« first showed me the rules of the house. Also, the godfather would accompany me through the entire therapy. As a new patient, I was accompanied from the start and not alone. At the beginning I had to visit the doctor of the clinic. This one assessed me in my person in order to record this status at the beginning of the therapy. I was still very insecure in this status. But I saw how many of the fellow clients, sometimes more and sometimes less, were coping with the therapy. I saw in their faces that behind one or the other facade it was bubbling or crumbling. In detox, I decided not to focus on whether others would make it.

 I gave myself the gift of a fresh start through my decision. There was early morning exercise every morning, which everyone completed. Then there was breakfast, followed by a big round of talks in a large room. Mostly led by two therapists. Already here it became clear who took the therapy seriously or tried to muddle through. Was someone wiggling their chair? Was someone obviously whispering to his neighbor? All these little disrespectful actions were recorded by the therapists. Whether you rated them or not was not known. Here, issues were raised that were everybody's business. Who had broken which rules? Who got what consequence for what? A consequence could also mean a transfer to a correctional facility. Because the person didn't want to change even though they could. There was always an elected deputy for all clients. This person had the task of addressing issues that wanted to be discussed on behalf of all. If someone had caught someone else breaking a rule, they wrote it down on a piece of paper. And then threw it into a »bump box«. So every violation was a »bump«. These bumps were read out in the morning by the SV (client in a role of a supervisor for the clients) outside in the smoking room or inside in the living room.

Depending on the offense, there is of course sometimes heated discussion. Due to everyone's previous history, there were sometimes attempts to manipulate each other based on their own interests. This was the real life. To see how violently clients lied to themselves and tricked around was very instructive. But it was also not pretty, because one should always keep in mind: Everyone's livelihoods were at stake here. The therapists exposed themselves to fierce situations on a daily basis. So there were also clients who already had many, had served many years in prison. The addiction in one's own head played a huge role here, of course. Would one remain stable? How many attempts at manipulation could one resist?

The therapy offered many possibilities. There was generally a daily program, planned down to the minute, which had to be completed. If one was one minute late, it was noticed and possibly punished. It was hard, but it was fair (like that Intro from movie »Full Metal Jacket«). The program was not always the same. For example, the program changed from a longer group discussion to a round of relaxation. And there were always enough breaks in between. At the beginning of the therapy, it was strange to feel now »just relax«. For many clients, this state was difficult to endure, especially at the beginning of the therapy. So they turned around, twitched, puffed or became really restless just when they were supposed to become calm.

Understandable for people who otherwise partied for days on heavy drugs. In essence, it was a matter of sensibly aligning therapy in two directions: Body and mind. Through sports or relaxation, one did something for the body on a regular basis. By talking about one's own or other people's issues, one did something for the mind. I felt that the mixture of both directions was very coherent here. So the structure did not have only »one way«. There were many small paths, but they all led to the right destination. For me, the analysis of my own life story was very crucial. So after a few conversations I saw that I had taken myself hostage for years in my role as a victim. I couldn't imagine the freedom of all the beer cans. It was like you can't see the forest because of all the trees. It was incredibly liberating to suddenly have completely new views and perspectives in front of me.

The therapists who really listened to you and also understood. The people who truly care about helping people find themselves. To get back on the right path. That inspired me. Little by little, my personal path through this therapy developed. In the later course there was also again the possibility to maintain the contacts to the outside. The contact to my girlfriend broke off, which was understandable due to the distance and previous history. Of course I was sad about this for some time, but then I accepted this as a natural consequence and part of the path. However, the contact with my family could start fresh and new. I was very happy about this, especially since there was a lot that I could simply leave in the past. And for my family it was also very good and helpful. That was especially good. Positive therapy participation also made it possible for me to take part in joint outings to the city in the second half of the year. You went at least as a couple and when you returned you always had to take an alcohol test. After a year of inpatient therapy, I received my regular diploma, laminated in foil, in 2005. This meant not only a farewell to the therapists, but also a change of location from the inpatient facility on the mountain, down to the outskirts of the city. To the so-called adaption: the outpatient therapy part in a kind of shared apartment.

35. Outpatient therapy - resocialization

After moving to the adaption, I met new therapists and social workers there again. There, too, there was daily care and a night watch for possible emergencies. There were also single or double rooms. I lived in the whole time a two-bed room, which I could use mostly alone. My godfather, who had moved to the outpatient clinic some time before me, also welcomed me here. He showed me how to get to the for example a »Turkish Sucukpan« prepares. Very tasty! The adaptation was about about getting through school or vocational measures to integrate themselves into a social environment. Of course, there were also dropouts and relapses. That was and is completely normal in therapy. It was important to concentrate on oneself as much as possible and not to lose sight of one's own goals. Since this part was also part of the paid therapy, one did not have to worry about money for rent or living expenses. Pocket money was paid out at regular intervals. I was able to plan and start your career or school start in a relaxed manner. Here, too, there were group and individual discussions, but much less frequently. Family trips could also take place from here. After returning home, you were always tested for alcohol. Later just by chance. Drug tests were even rarer. As a career start, I initially chose a part-time job and caught up on my secondary school diploma at an evening school. At the end of the therapy I was able to move into a small apartment just one street away. And there I experienced a fun time on the edge of a problem district. Due to the place of residence, I also learned some Turkish words through the neighbors. I had funny, pleasant and also less pleasant neighbors. But on the whole I could start here very well from the beginning. My healthy time began. Finally I could start again from zero.

36. New beginning

This was followed by full-time jobs through various temporary employment agencies. Unfortunately, the financial and economic crisis of 2007 also made itself felt in Germany in 2008. I was able to get rid of my old financial burdens in the course of a private insolvency. After several attempts to apply for a job, I received an offer of employment before Christmas at the end of 2008. This time without a temporary employment agency. This was really good karma. The following spring I started my new job as an office help. This company sold consumables for printers. In this company I was taught how to talk to customers on the phone. There and in self-study I learned a lot about printers. The boss and the authorized signatory had a really, really great patience.

Until 2015, I learned a lot about the commercial area. At home, I practiced very disciplined with exam material. And on my own initiative, I took an external exam to become a commercial clerk for office management. I changed my place of residence and employer once again after I met my new girlfriend. The job changed first to customer service, then to working in shipping. After more than five years of mainly commercial work, I finally wanted to do some physical work. Privately, everything was going well. But I finally wanted to make my earlier dream of working with a computer a reality become. And after three years in shipping, I succeeded. In addition to my full-time job, I continued my education at my own expense. And in 2020, I passed an exam to become an IT specialist. And it wasn't long before I was able to land a job in the IT department through an internal job posting. In the end, I even managed to get my dream job.

37. Epilog

I am standing on the mountain in Schöningen and looking out into the horizon. It's great for me to be able to experience this moment. I often drive here and take a walk. I always walk the same way because the path means a healthy routine. I like to distinguish between rational or emotional thinking. To analyze myself and question if something is really necessary or not. What is it necessary or important for? What negative behaviors do I have and do I really want to change them at all? To what extent can I be a role model? Questioning my thinking is vital for me. I saw an x-ray of my brain with many white dots. Where nothing is anymore. My short-term memory has suffered extremely from years of use. If I want to memorize information, I have to consume it much more often to make it stick. If it were only that. People I've seen once or twice, my brain can't remember. In order for me to internalize the driving route to a certain place, I'm sure I have to drive that route five times. It scares me that I don't know the names of some people anymore. Or it takes a long time for this information to crawl back out of long-term memory. Yes, I am forgetful have become.

 But I have an armada of tools to counteract that. From my point of view, it is also important to stay with myself in the way I went down this path. That is, everyone must find his own way and want to go this way.

Respect yourself. I wish you, even if unknown: a family, strength and health.

Names of people and places have been changed, but the story is true.

Thank you for buying the book!

Jan Fogfrost

Note: This was my first attempt of a translation. If you wanna help me to correct this translation or want a contact to the real autor write an email to:

janfogfrost@mailbox.org